The Appalachian Collection

Remembering the Hill Country

By

Harold H. Milton

Requests for permission to make copies of any part of this work should be mailed to:
Janice L. Blanton
376 Canterbury Road
Bay Village, Ohio 44140

ISBN-13: 978-1625503404
ISBN-10: 1625503407

Printed in the United States of America
Printed by Janice Publishing

Harold H. Milton, died in 1998. He was born in 1913.

It is therefore that I, Janice L. Blanton, speak for my Dad

to complete his dreams. Harold was generous to those

who were down on their luck and it was life's obligations

prevented him from the publishing of his writings of 40 years. I,

Janice, dedicate this book to my mother, Nellie Agnes Romeo

Blanton, 1924-1960, my father Orville, 1922-1966, Harold's

wife, Jane, 1925-1986, his daughter, Nancy, 1950-1970, his

parents, Eva, 1885-1963, Charles, 1872-1946, grandfather

Marion, 1845-1920,who fought in the civil war. His siblings are

Hazel, Myrtle, Jewell, and Mary, my dear friend, Robert F.

Burkhardt, and the Church of Christ and to myself,

Janice Louise Blanton.

Acknowledgment

Harold H. Milton's first book, Mountain Dew, was completed after twelve years while he was writing other novels and short stories. He began his ideas in the 1930's. He was German and born in Marietta, Ohio December 23rd, 1913, the only red haired son of Charles Henry Milton born February 10th, 1872 and whom passed away November 22, 1946 and Eva Marilla Farley born January 6th, 1885 and passing away April 1963. He had three older Sisters named Hazel, Myrtle, Jewell and one younger named Mary. They lived in a small cabin and had their education in a one room school house. Their poverty was severe and Harold was embarrassed to carry all five lunches to school in a basket. During the depression, Harold had to quit school in the eighth grade to help his Father with farming and hunt Ginseng and Yellowroot for profit. Together they traveled for many days throughout the vast woods of West Virginia. There were many attempts to move there as they had pushed a covered wagon but the wheels would get stuck in the mud or the wagon broke down. Harold loved these times with his Father and they would have contests to see who would find the most herbs. Harold moved to Cleveland, Ohio in his twenties and married Jane A. Romeo from West Virginia. Jane was born October 3rd, 1925 of Dutch, Italian and English descent. He worked for White Motors. She passed away December 1986.

It was a cold blizzardy day when I, Janice Louise Blanton was born in Cleveland, Ohio on January 16th, 1955 to Nellie Agnes Romeo who was born February 1st, 1924 in Gypsy, West Virginia and Orville B. Blanton born July 18th, 1922 in Kentucky. The rule at Booth Memorial, a Salvation Army Hospital for unwed Mothers was that you could live there your last trimester, you had to do chores and you had to relinquish your baby. Nellie took me home and my first crib was a dresser drawer for five months. She then married Orville and continued her waitress job while Harold and Jane babysat me for four months on. Five years later, my Mother, Nellie died of Leukemia at 36 years of age and Harold agreed to raise me full time while my Father, Orville, visited often until he died in 1966 at 43 years old of heart disease.

In 1960, Harold knocked on many doors and built a congregation to open a Church of Christ. We spend weekends walking thru the woods collecting Ginseng that dried out in our attic and was sold. He loved to talk about his childhood days and speak German with his Daughter, Nancy, who also died at nineteen years old of a brain tumor while in her second year of Cleveland State University. She was a lovely red head and we loved each other as Sisters and laughed a lot and played tennis. The feeling of my being orphaned kept getting worse but Harold was there for me and it made us closer to be Father and Daughter. As children, Nancy and I were asked by him, "What do you girls want when my books hit big?" Her answer was a white baby grand piano.

For forty years, he wrote and typed books that were wanted for publishing in New York. He never had the finances for this and Nancy's college loans and funeral expenses were high, though he continued writing.

With my encouragement, he completed his G.E.D. at 79 years old. I had a nice party and it made the newspaper. He planned to go to College but we moved to a different home further away. He always wanted to see the Grand Canyon so in 1994, we went there. We stayed

in Vegas. He always liked that also and would imitate a robot dancing

that he had seen in a show. He died at eighty four years old as I held

his hand in the hospital. I was an emergency room Registered Nurse

working all departments, however, up to 100 hours a week. As I

watched Harold's passing, I was saddened that his departing was such

as loss, for he knew his Bible word for word and was so generous,

kind and smart.I inspired to become a Nurse at age eight and had taken

care of him when he was very sick before and after surgery in 1963.

He had taken care of me also. Around 2000, I noticed his books under

my stairwell and read some of it, however in 2013, I wanted to get

them published and leave his fingerprint in the world.

It is now through my labor of love that I present to you the

writings of my second Father Harold Homer Milton. As I now carry

out his dream and pull back the curtain of time and the past, he smiles

down from heaven and becomes a known author. I can now sit back

and listen to Nancy play on her white baby grand piano. His five books

are named *Mountain Dew*, *The Treasure of the Hills*, *Water Baptism*,

The Conquest of Lonnie Dolan and *The Appalachian Collection: Remembering the Hill Country.*

Fondly and with great honor,

Janice Louise Blanton

Table of Contents

The Root of All Evil

Chapter 1

The stars were still shining that October morning in 1896 when Seth Henderson and his family hitched up and started for Camden, Ohio, to sell their tobacco crop. Their wagon and the one they had borrowed from a neighbor were piled high with bundles of bright golden tobacco leaves that were bound up in "hands." Old quilts covered the contents of both vehicles.

Seth and his wife, Amy, rode atop the lead wagon. Their sons, Charles,

George, and Silas, brought up the rear with the borrowed one. As they drove along, Seth complained to his patient, long-suffering wife about the injustices of life, and of tobacco buyers in general.

"Damn it all to hell, Amy," he said, flicking the long, snake-like horsewhip over the backs of the straining horses. "Reckon I'm slated to have that dirty Jack Hines skin me outta most of my tobacco crop again."

"Maybe he'll do better by you this time," Mrs. Henderson ventured, trying as all good wives do to placate her fuming husband.

"Aw, balls, woman" was his disgusted retort. "You know better than that. I'm expectin' that son of a bitch to show his scales more this time than ever. He's slicker than a greased pig, an' crooked as a copperhead snake. Be prepared for us to take another peelin'. I feel it's in the cards."

"Let's hope not," she said patiently. "Leastwise keep faith that it won't. All things comes to them that wait, they say. Perhaps the Good Lord will see fit to shorten our waiting time."

"My faith has grown dim," Seth grumbled as he remembered some of the crushing disappointments life had handed him. "Come next spring I'll pass the half century mark—an' I'm still grubbing fer a living fer me an' my family. If you ask me, there just ain't no justice in this life."

The heavily laden wagons rolled on. As mile after mile passed under the iron-rimmed wheels, signs of weariness began to show on both man and beast. The weather had been drought-like that fall, so the turning wheels churned up dust from the dirt road. The dust hung like a pall over the slow-moving vehicles. Soon a heavy film of it covered the wagons and their passengers. Then it began to cake on the straining horses where it mixed with their lathered sweat.

Every now and then the Hendersons would encounter people they didn't know coming from the opposite direction. Seth and his wife would speak pleasantly to them, as they had not seen strangers in months.

It was high noon when they reached their destination. Camden, Ohio, was a typical rural village. Nevertheless, it differed from others of equal size in some respects. A jerkwater railroad touched there. Also, the village housed two general stores, a blacksmith, a barber, a doctor, and last, but not least, a tobacco buyer.

As was his wont, Seth Henderson endeavored to drive his wagons as close to the buyer's packing house as possible before unhitching the horses. This, he had difficulty in accomplishing. After more than half an hour of fruitless driving around, he located a spot that, though not to his liking, would have to do until he could find one closer in. Tobacco-laden wagons lined the streets on both sides. He and his sons had no sooner seen to the needs of the weary horses than they were greeting old friends and acquaintances they had not seen since the fall before.

"How's crops over your way?" Seth inquired of a tall, leathery-faced farmer who lived ten miles away on Crane's Nest Creek. Jed Sloan had once run a farm next to Seth's. But since his wife's death, Jed had made his home with a married daughter in Crane's Nest.

"Fair to middlin', I guess," Jed Sloan replied as he shook hands with the Hendersons. "Especially the tobaccer. All us raisers on Crane's Nest had bumper crops of the weed this year. But from the ways things look, we've had our efforts for naught." He spat a brown stream of tobacco juice from between his whiskered lips.

"How so?" Seth asked.

"Tobaccer's taken a slump. That's how so."

"What is Hines paying?" Mrs. Henderson asked hesitantly.

"Two cents less on the pound than last year."

Seth swore. "By the eternal," he snarled, balling his huge hands into fists. "Hines might skin me like a stiff jock this fall, but I'll be *damned* if he'll ever do it again."

"How're you aimin' on preventin' it?" Jed Sloan asked.

"Refuse to sell to him. That's what I'll do. And if necessary, I'll mortgage the old homestead to keep from givin' my crop away."

"Pa, you wouldn't," Charles cried. "Remember what happened to Tom Winlin? He tried to buck the buyers and he ended up losin' his home and everything."

At their brother's words, Silas and George gaped at their father. Knowing his dogged determination when riled, they could picture nothing but disaster should he decide to rebel against the accepted order of things.

"Enough of yer long faces and dark predictions," Seth growled to his sons and wife. "That's one bridge we'll cross when we come to it.

"Thanks fer putting me wise, Jed," he said, turning to his former neighbor. "At least I now know what to expect from Hines. Come on, Amy. Boys. Let's get some wet packin' under our belts before we give our tobaccer away fer a song."

Jed Sloan's information proved correct. At two o'clock that afternoon, Jack Hines stepped out onto the loading platform of his packing house and announced to the score or more of tight-lipped men before him that, due to an unforeseen slump in the market, he would be forced to pay two cents less per pound of tobacco that fall than he had the previous year.

"Men," he said, "it grieves me to have to do this. But my pocketbook is not fat enough to permit sentiment to enter into the picture. Either I buy your tobacco at a price where I can make a reasonable profit on it—or I'm out of business. It's as simple as that. Should any of you feel that what I've told you is unsatisfactory, then the railroad here at Camden is at your disposal. Of course, if I store your tobacco in my packing house until you can arrange shipment to Cincinnati, I'll naturally expect reimbursement for my time and trouble. Think it over. My meal is waiting for me. I mean to weigh up your crops within the hour, should you decide to sell to me."

Immediately after his announcement Hines stepped back inside his packing house and closed the door. A half hour of heated arguments ensued among the farmers. Tempers flared against what they all knew was a slick way to relieve them of their tobacco crops at a portion of their worth. Some of the younger men seriously considered not selling that year at all.

"It's robbery," one shouted. "That's what it is. An' that two-legged skunk knows that we know it too." The others agreed loudly.

"Easy neighbors," the older heads counseled. Theirs was the wisdom of speech and action that comes of living long hard years.

"We know what's happenin'," one shouted, using his silvery position to dicker for calm. The others nodded in agreement. "Winter will soon be here. Even if we decide to ship our crops to Cincinnati, he's got us over a barrel. First, he can refuse to let us use his packing house to store our tobacco in until shipment can be arranged. Second, even if he does let us

20

use it, he can charge the pants off us an' we can't do a thing but pay through the nose. We say *sell*. An' hope fer a better deal next season."

"All right," Seth Henderson shouted, righteous indignation written on his craggy features. He raised his arms above his head to emphasize his next words. "I won't hold up the deal this time. But next year? I'm singin' a different tune. I want the hand of every man jack of you present that come next fall you'll sell me yer tobaccer. If you promise to sell to me, I promise I'll pay more than any buyer you can haul to in a long day's travel in any direction. Next year it's gonna be sink or swim with me. An' another thing. I'll pay off in gold if you sell to me. No more due bills in stores that always charges us two prices fer their stale rotten junk."

Before the discussions broke up that afternoon, every farmer present shook the hand of Seth Henderson and pledged to sell his next year's tobacco crop to him, should he decide to buy. Thus it came about that Seth was thrust into the tobacco-buying business by the cruel hand of fate.

Chapter 2

The following year, Seth Henderson made good on his promise to his neighbors. Not only did he raise more tobacco than ever before on his own land, but he also mortgaged his ancestral home to purchase the crops that had been pledged to him the previous year. But fate once again saw fit to deal him a cruel blow.

As marketing time drew near, the price of tobacco sank lower and lower. Then, when only one month remained until the delivery of his neighbors' crops, word came from a large buyer in Cincinnati, Ohio, that bottom had virtually dropped out of the tobacco market. When he read this crushing news, Seth came to the full realization that he faced financial ruin. Thereafter the specter of foreclosure was his constant companion during all his waking hours. It even haunted his dreams.

Even though his trials and anxieties were many and grievous, he despaired not. Instead, he stood proudly, as a rugged forest monarch, and steadfastly refused to be swayed from his purpose. When his neighbors said, "Forget yer promise to buy our tobaccer this season," he turned a deaf ear to them and replied, "I'll abide by your word."

And on a clear, cool October day in 1897, he bought all his neighbors' tobacco and paid for every ounce of it with gold coin.

"Friends, neighbors," he said with pardonable pride tempering his deep voice that day, "I've kept my word, as I promised. Now I'm askin' fer another pledge from every one of you fer the comin' year. I may go under. But if I can git a second mortgage on all my land an' stock, I want yer tobaccer crop next season too. I ain't gonna sell any this fall. I figger on holdin' it all till next year. Then I'll try to unload it at a bit of profit. I've enough room in my barn an' outbuilding to store it. Do I have yer word—as men of yer word—to sell to me again next season?"

"You do, Seth," they solemnly agreed. But knowing the financial burden he already carried and the worry that stalked him, they consideredit the rankest kind of foolhardiness for him to contract new liens against his property; and they told him as much.

24

"Seth," one said, "just what in hell are you trying to do? At the rate you're goin', by the time next fall rolls around, you an' Amy will be in the county house."

"We're not there yet," he replied, his lips set in a grim line. "I wouldn't bet any of you though that we won't wind up there. But that's a chance I figger I might as well take. I'm in debt over my head as it is. Getting the second loan what's got me worried. I started my business career by payin' off in gold. I want to keep it up, if I can."

"What about Jack Hines?" a dour-faced farmer from over on Straight Fork asked.

"To hell with him," Seth growled. "Long as I can keep my head above water, I ain't fer letting that no-good snake cheat any of you out of an ounce of yer tobaccer."

"What's he doin' this year?" another asked.

"Nothing much, far as I can find out," Seth informed them.

"The story goin' around is that he's bought in with one of the general stores in Camden. They say he's payin' fer what tobaccer he buys with due bills on the store," one man said.

"That sounds like Hines's kind of dealin'," Jed Sloan muttered.

"Sure does," Seth agreed, his blood running hot at the thought of how the man had shortchanged him in the past. "Trust that son of a bitch to figger out a sweet setup fer himself. I only hope we'll all be able to steer clear of his lousy schemes in the future."

"Look, men," Bill Harmon, owner of an adjoining farm, said. "The way I see it, Seth is takin' all the risk in this tobaccer buyin' plan."

"How so, Bill?" another neighbor asked.

"Well, he's mortgaging the very shirt on his back to raise the money to do this favor fer us. Now suppose we make our promise to him as bindin' as his obligation is gonna be to the bank that holds the liens on his property."

"Explain yourself," someone said.

"All right, here's my idea. Let's draw up an agreement that's bindin' on us as well as Seth. We'll all sign it, an' all keep a copy. That way there won't be any of us able to welch on our promise should tobaccer take a big jump in price 'tween now an' next fall—which ain't likely. What do you men think of the idea?"

"Old friend," Seth said, "I appreciate yer interest in tryin' to protect me. But I ain't overly fond of signin' something that'd put my friends over a barrel. Just yer word alone is good enough fer me."

"Let's let the men decide," Bill Harmon said. The men talked the idea over among themselves, then selected Bill to talk for them. "We insist," he informed Seth. "An' to show our good intentions, we've all agreed to ask fer no more than a ten percent increase on the price you paid us this year, which was quite a bit over the present market price. How does that sound to you, Seth?"

"More than fair," he muttered, trying to find words to express his appreciation for their thoughtfulness. "I'll sign the paper if yer sure that's the way it's got be. But you needn't, you know. I ain't askin' a scratch of a pen of any of you."

"Okay then, it's settled," Bill Harmon said, smiling. "Tomorrow I'll see Squire Johnson and have him draw up the agreement. Also, I'll have him make a copy fer each of us. That way we'll all know where we stand in our obligation to Seth."

Within a fortnight, Seth Henderson possessed a paper that legally bound every one of them to sell him their tobacco again the following year, regardless of the price per pound by then.

That evening as he relaxed after supper and smoked his pipe, he talked with his wife about the agreement he had signed that afternoon with his neighbors. Had he been able to foresee the startling developments that the next twelve months would bring to his financial status, he would have doubted his sanity.

"They're all good men, Amy," he said, his deep voice slightly shaking. "Yes indeed. They're all good as gold. I sincerely hope I'll be able to keep their faith in me from growin' dim. The way I see it, a man's just got to be on the level with his friends. Otherwise, he ain't much of a man."

As usual, Amy Henderson quietly agreed with her husband. Rising from the huge armchair he was sitting in, Seth began preparing to retire for the night. Good wife that she was, Amy shared her husband's doubts and fears about what the uncertain future could do to their security. Worried sick though she was, she nonetheless resolved to be cheerful and encouraging at all times. Never, in any way, would she parade her anxieties. Hers would be a suffering of silence. Even through her tears, she vowed that she would succeed in hiding her troubled thoughts from her husband.

···

The following winter fate once again interfered in the lives of the Hendersons. At the time, relations between the United States and Spain had been strained for several months. Then, on February 15, 1898, the hostilities began in earnest after the United States battleship *Maine* was accidentally blown up in Havana Harbor.

Two months later, almost to the day, war was declared. First by Spain, and a day later by the United States.

Shortly after open hostilities began between the two nations, the prices of all commodities began a rapid climb. By midsummer, practically every item on the open market had more than doubled in valuation. Needless to say, the price of tobacco followed suit.

The conflict between the United States and Spain lasted a little less than four months. John Hay, an ambassador at the time to the United Kingdom, would best be remembered as the man who described the conflict as "a splendid little war."

During the summer of 1898, Seth Henderson underwent a mental about-face on all pertaining to dealing with one's fellow man. The transformation of his thinking was so gradual that he was completely unaware that anything out of the ordinary was happening to him. The first day he became aware that he had had a change of heart was when his neighbor Bill Harmon dropped by after church one Sunday afternoon with a two-day-old newspaper under his arm. Seth had been dozing on his front porch.

"Howdy, Bill," he greeted his life-long friend. "Come up on the porch outta that hot sun an' set yourself down."

"Don't mind if I do," Bill replied, giving Seth a hard look as he did so. "That old sun is hot this afternoon, an' no mistake. How's yer crops doin'? Corn about ripe?"

"Crops is good all over this year, Bill," Seth answered. "Another two weeks of this heat an' I'll be cutting my corn. That is if it stays dry."

"Me too."

"I didn't git to raise as much this season as I'd of liked to. Charley bein' away with the army sort of left me shorthanded. He's only eighteen, but they took him just the same. My tobaccer crop ain't as big this year as it should be either."

"Speaking of, Seth," Bill said, eyeing his neighbor closely, "have you seen a newspaper lately?"

"No. But I heard last week that the war's over. That's good enough news to me. Reckon the boys will soon be home. It's been a long six months since my boy left for camp."

"Same here," Bill said dryly. "But that ain't what I was referring to."

"Oh, I suppose you mean the way things are lookin' up this summer." Seth laughed and cast a sidelong glance at his old friend. Bill was watching him with a peculiar look on his face.

"That's right," he said. "While we're on the subject, have you received any quotations on the price of tobaccer within the last two weeks?"

"Can't say that I have." But in his heart, Seth knew he was telling a barefaced lie to a life-long friend. Only the day before, he had received a letter from a large wholesaler in Cincinnati stating that tobacco was selling close to three times what it had per pound the fall before.

"That's funny," Bill Harmon said. He removed the newspaper from under his arm and pointed to an item on the front page. "It say there, Seth, that right now tobaccer is selling fer about three times what it sold fer last fall. How about that?"

"They could be wrong," Seth muttered, wiping an unusual amount of sweat off his brow. "The market time ain't fer two months yet, Bill. Anything could happen before then."

"Don't tell me yer lookin' fer a drop in price?" Bill said with a cutting edge in his voice.

"Not especially," Seth said, getting angry at his old friend's pointed questions. "Bill, what in hell is this? Why the third degree?"

"Don't you know?"

"No, I don't," he snapped, but he was unable to meet his friend's eyes.

"Want me to spell it out fer you?"

"I don't foller you, Bill."

"All right, Seth, if that's the way you want it. Here it is, short an' sweet. You know as well as I do that you're goin' to make a purty penny on the tobaccer us fellers sold you last fall. Fact is, it'll bring a premium price right now."

"I know all that," Seth acknowledged, shuffling his feet from side to side in his agitation.

"Therefore, knowing all this," Bill said, "I've a little proposition to put to you, in all fairness to yerself an' yer neighbors, that is. Want to hear it?"

At the question, a steely glint sprang into Seth Henderson's eyes. He stared at his life-long friend as though he had suddenly become a total stranger. In turn, Bill paled and lowered his eyes.

"Seth," he said, his eyes still downcast, "I know this ain't a proper day to talk business, it being Sunday an' all, but I thought you wouldn't mind too much, considerin' we've been friends an' neighbors all our lives."

"Come to the point, Bill," Seth said in a voice he no longer recognized as his own.

"Since you ask me that way, reckon I'll have to," Bill muttered. "The truth is, me an' some of the fellers happened to meet over at Camden the other afternoon an' had ourselves a gab fest. The fellers ain't happy, Seth. Considerin' the way the prices have jumped, they appointed me a one-man committee to ask you to tear up that paper all of us signed last fall.

32

"Now I ain't sayin' it ain't perfectly legal, an' all that," he hurried on. "But, as it is, you'll git three times over what you paid fer the tobaccer we sold you last fall. That ain't a bad profit in any man's language. So we all agreed it'd be only fair to us, as yer neighbors, to forget any agreement we had. It ain't been exactly easy on any of us these past two years. You know that, Seth. Now what do you say?"

"Did I forget my promise to you fellers last fall?" Seth said sharply.

"No, you didn't," Bill admitted. "But remember, we told you to. Knowin' how hard-pressed all of us was at the time, we wouldn't have thought bad of you if you'd refused to buy even an ounce of our tobaccer. Seth, listen to me. Us fellers ain't tryin' to welch on our agreement. Pay us the present market price. That's all we're askin'. Ain't that fair enough?"

"No," Seth Henderson roared, like a man suddenly gone berserk. Springing out of his chair, he confronted his old friend with a passion-twisted face that bore no resemblance to the Seth Henderson of other days. In that terrible moment, Bill Harmon realized he no longer knew the man before him.

"Go back to them yeller-bellies an' tell them this," Seth said savagely. "You're all goin' to live up to the agreement we signed. Every last word of it. An' I don't mean perhaps. Try any monkey business an' I'll have the lot

33

of you in court. I ain't payin' you birds one red cent more than we agreed on. That's my final word."

"But, Seth," Bill Harmon cried, "we're all yer friends. Don't you realize that?"

"Gold is my friend, my only friend. Now git off my property before I throw you off. When you show yer face around here again, you'd best have yer tobaccer. I'm buyin' this fall, Harmon. Buyin' from all you fellers like we agreed in writin'. Either that, or I'll sue you crawfishin' rats till hell freezes over an' you can skate on the ice. Now go—go!"

Like a man unwilling to believe what he had just seen and heard, Bill Harmon rose from his chair and walked off the porch.

Through the open windows, Amy Henderson overheard her husband order his old friend away. Shaking her head in hopeless resignation, the good woman returned to her cleaning. What she had feared for months had finally come to pass.

That evening as they prepared for bed, Amy tried to dissuade her husband from the road he had chosen to follow. Perhaps, she reasoned, if she pleaded with him then he could be persuaded to change his mind before it was too late. She might as well have tried to turn the tide of the Ohio River when it was in flood. Seth Henderson was as immovable in his stand.

"No, Amy, no!" he yelled. "I'm havin' my just dues this fall. The agreement was their idea in the first place. Now I'm holdin' 'em to it. Ain't no wrong in that, now is there?"

"Forget this madness, husband," she implored. "If you insist on buying their tobacco, please pay them the market price. That's the least you can do."

"Never," he said sharply. "That tobaccer represents a heap of gold, an' I mean to have it."

"Please, I beg of you. Think of your position in the community, your family. Then think of these men. They're all your old friends and neighbors. Every one of them. No amount of gold in this world is worth the loss of that."

"Enough of yer damn preachin'," he said with his face set like a block of granite. "I want no more of it. From here on in, till they put me in a box, I'm puttin' my trust in something worthwhile. These past two years I've learned a hard lesson. Gold is what talks when the chips are down. Now you hear this, woman, an' hear it good. Give me the gold an' I'll buy a ten-acre field full of them fair-weather friends you've been yappin' about. Show me a bum an' I'll show you a man who ain't got one measly friend in this whole rotten world. An' only because he's broke. That's the way the chips fall, wife. It's a hard life, an' it's gospel truth. Now shut yer trap. I'm hittin' the hay."

Two months later Seth Henderson bought the tobacco crop of every man who had signed his name to the agreement they had drawn up the fall before. He threatened court against any who should fail to comply with the exact specifications of said agreement. As a result, he purchased every crop of tobacco for less than a third of its present market value. The returns from this cold-hearted transaction made him a financially independent man in the community. But it also made his neighbors and their families hate him for the rest of his natural life. So because of his greed for gold, Seth Henderson became a social outcast.

Chapter 3

During the next five years tobacco raising, as a money crop, diminished sharply. By the end of 1903, less than a third of its former production appeared on the local market. Many farmers ceased raising it altogether, except for home use, and switched to cattle as a means of future revenue.

Consequently, men who had formerly operated primarily as tobacco buyers were forced to turn their hands to more lucrative enterprises. Seth Henderson was no exception.

With his usual business acumen he quickly sensed the trend and, closing out his tobacco-purchasing activities, began speculating in real estate and cattle. Good fortune continued to smile on him. It was as though he possessed the Midas touch. Everything he put his hands to returned him a handsome profit.

He would purchase an old, rundown farm at a giveaway price, put a cheap coat of paint on the building, trim the brush off the fields, build a hundred dollars' worth of new fences on it, and then sell the farm for at least a thousand dollars more than he put into it.

In time, his real-estate speculations expanded to the point where he felt he needed a partner. He considered taking his sons into business with him. But after sounding them out, he quickly abandoned the idea. The type of partner he was interested in would have to be levelheaded in all business dealings; he would permit sentiment to play no part whatsoever in the purchase, conditioning, and sale of a property, regardless of whose toes might be stepped on in the process. There was a mint to be made in real estate, Seth knew, providing one had the cash to speculate on and an ambitious, unscrupulous partner to work with.

Eventually, he found a man who possessed these qualifications in abundance. James Moore ran a real-estate brokerage in Woodsfield, Ohio. And his reputation was unsavory, to say the least. When it came to unscrupulous methods of turning a deal to his advantage, he had few equals.

After a careful investigation of Moore's brokerage and financial standing, Seth entered into full partnership with him. Again, good fortune smiled on his efforts. And gold coins continued to flow to him in an uninterrupted stream.

At the onset of their business venture, Seth made it very clear to his new partner that he would accept no other medium of exchange for any and all transactions they would have together. "Gold is gold," he said, absolute conviction in his deep voice. "No man can take away its value. But paper money? Bah. It may be good today an' not worth the paper it's wrote on tomorrow. I'll accept none of it in payment, Moore. Remember that."

By this time, Seth was in his mid-fifties. Through the years he had enjoyed good health, and he still retained the bodily vigor that he'd had in his late thirties. But his wife's health was poor. And of late years, she had insisted they occupy separate bedrooms.

Consequently, many were the nights when his sexual desires were at a fever pitch with no gratification in sight, for he knew his wife wanted no part of his lovemaking. Amy Henderson, on the other hand, had never been generously endowed with the need for frequent sexual encounters. The small amount of passion she possessed had dissipated during menopause, so once the nervousness and hot flashes left her, Seth found her about as satisfying to indulge in the sex act with as a dead fish. Nor did she try to remedy this unwholesome condition between them in any way.

Their social standing among their former friends and neighbors was a far cry from what it had been. This, she knew, was the result of her husband's business ethics, and, because of his ethics—or rather, his lack of them—she had alienated herself against him. Added to this feeling of resentment were the infirmities of advancing age. The result was that they'd reached the stage in their married life that is termed in divorce courts as "total incompatibility." So it was that Seth Henderson began seeking sexual satisfaction elsewhere.

...

In the spring of 1906, at the insistence of his business partner, Seth took a passenger boat to the Deep South to explore the possibility of investing in some well-situated and developed property in a sunnier clime.

Real-estate values had begun to skyrocket in and around New Orleans and certain sections of Florida. Being an aggressive and farsighted man, James Moore wanted in on the ground floor of any real-estate boom that might develop in these sections.

During the six weeks he was on the trip, Seth had numerous occasions to sample the wares being peddled by the beautiful wantons who made the passenger boats on the river their hunting grounds.

But his association with these lovely young women proved to be far from satisfying. Physically, they were perfection itself. And that was where their appeal to him soon ended. Their primary objective at all times was the acquisition of money, nothing else. To them, the sex act was purely a mechanical affair from beginning to end. They gave no signs of real enjoyment during copulation.

"You burned-out bitches," he said in disgust after he had indulged in sexual relations with more than one of them. "Foolin' with the likes of you is a waste of time an' money. I'm headin' fer home on the next passenger boat north."

Cutting his trip short by two weeks, he sailed for Ohio, a thoroughly disillusioned man.

■■■

One Saturday afternoon of the following summer, in mid-July, Seth was traveling by horse and buggy along a high ridge on a back county road in the southeastern part of Monroe County. He was investigating a hot real-estate tip that had come into the office the week before.

The ridges and domes along the narrow dirt road were like mountains and provided a bit of scenic grandeur. They swept up and up from deep, dark wooded hollows that sloped away from the ridge-like canyons.

Rounding a sharp bend, he saw two small children dart across the road about a hundred feet ahead of him. Soon after, he saw a log cabin with a lean-to kitchen attached to it nestled in a small cove on the upper side of the road.

The day was hot and humid, and he was thirsty. As he came abreast of the cabin, he drew rein. Perhaps, he thought, I could get myself a cool drink of water here.

"Whoa, hoss," he said to his horse as he climbed out of the buggy. Once on the ground, he tied the animal to a post on one of the yard fences. The children he had seen earlier were nowhere in sight.

"Anybody home?" he called, opening the gate and stepping into the yard. At his call, the deep baying of a hound sounded from behind the cabin; it was followed by the rattle of a chain.

The cabin door swung open and a dark-haired woman stepped out onto the small front porch. The two children Seth had seen crossing the road tugged at her faded gingham dress.

"Howdy, ma'am," Seth said pleasantly, removing his hat. "Sure is hot today. I thought maybe I could trouble you fer a drink of well water."

42

"Why certainly," she said with a smile. "Come sit on the porch out of the sun, and I'll draw up a fresh bucket in a jiffy."

"Thank you," he said. "But don't go to a lot of bother. Just show me the well. I'll draw it up."

"Please sit down, sir," she insisted. "Drawing water is one of the easiest tasks I have."

Stepping back inside, she soon came out carrying a galvanized bucket. A moment later she disappeared around the edge of the cabin and Seth heard the rattling of a windlass.

Seating himself on the edge of the porch, he leaned back against one of its posts. After giving him a couple of round-eyed looks, the little boy and girl trotted out into the yard and resumed their playing across the dirt road.

The woman reappeared a moment later with a dripping bucket of water. Setting it beside him, she handed him a dipper made from a large gourd.

"Help yourself, sir," she said, seating herself on the porch steps. "It's a limestone water, but it's good."

Smiling his thanks, Seth dipped the gourd into the clear water and offered the dripping cup to her.

"Oh. Please, no," she said laughing and waving the cup away. "Do help yourself. I drank some at the well."

The water was very satisfying, Seth soon discovered. Its clear-cold goodness quickly quenched his burning thirst. After two cups, he leaned back against the porch post again and gave a sigh of real relief.

"Ah, but that was good," he said with a grin. "It sure hit the spot. If you don't mind, ma'am, I'd like to rest a spell before goin' on. It's awful nice and relaxin' here in the shade of yer porch."

"You're welcome to rest as long as you want to, sir," she said, raising a hand to brush a strand of dark hair back from her brow. "Aren't you a stranger to these parts, though? I don't recollect ever seeing you before."

"My name's Henderson, ma'am. Seth Henderson. An' you're right. This part of Monroe County is new to me. Fact of the matter is, I lost my way this afternoon. Perhaps you could tell me where I've wandered to."

"I'm very happy to make your acquaintance, Mr. Henderson," she said with a smile. "I'm Ellie Morrison. If you'll tell me where you wanted to get in the first place, maybe I can set you straight."

"Be glad to. I'm part owner of a real-estate brokerage in Woodsfield. Last week we heard of a farm down this way that can be bought for a reasonable price. This morning I started out to take a look at it. Seems like I took a wrong turn back a ways."

"Perhaps so," she agreed. "What farm were you interested in?"

"The old Murdock place. Does it lay around here?"

"Yes, it does," she replied, laughing at the way he looked at the surrounding hills. "These old hills are something to figure out, I'll admit. They don't bother me much anymore, though. I suppose it's because I've lived most of my life looking at them. The Murdock place is down at the mouth of a hollow that empties into Perkins Run."

"Can I get there by this road?"

"Yes," she said, stepping off the porch steps and pointing to a ridge. "Out ahead there, about a mile or so, this road drops down into the valleys. You'll hit the county road there. Turn right, and about half a mile up Perkins Run, you'll come to the Murdock place."

"Who's livin' there now?" Seth asked.

"Nobody. It's been vacant for over a year. Getting run down quite a bit too, standing idle like that."

"Uh-huh, I see. Pardon my askin', ma'am, but what, besides farmin', does yer husband do fer a livin'?"

At his question, she reseated herself on the porch steps and looked at him with big dark eyes shadowed with pain.

"I have no husband," she whispered sadly, twisting her apron into a

45

ball in her lap.

"Oh, I'm sorry, ma'am," Seth said. "I really didn't mean to pry into yer personal life. It was only curiosity that made me ask. But now I reckon I got to ask you another question. What happened to yer man? Don't tell me he walked out on you an' these little children?"

"Oh, God, no," she said. "Ted loved me and the kids. He got killed in a coal mine cave-in up close to Powhatan Point. T-two years ago last month." She burst into tears and covered her face with shaking hands.

Seth quickly stepped to her side and laid a hand on her shoulder. He felt a tremor run through her body, but she made no move to dislodge his hand.

"I'm awfully sorry I opened my big mouth, Mrs. Morrison," he said. "Please forgive me. It's too bad about yer husband. Reckon I better leave before I stick my nose into yer business anymore."

"It's all right, Mr. Henderson," she said, raising her head and wiping her eyes on her apron. "How was you to know? If you'll stay, I'll fix a bit of supper. Ted always said to feed the strangers that came to our door. I don't have anything fancy to put on the table, but you're welcome to what I've got."

"Ma'am, you make me awful ashamed," Seth muttered, feeling uncomfortable at the way her sorry plight and grief had affected him.

"What about you an' the kids, since yer man's gone?" he felt compelled to ask. "How've you been getting along? I know from experience that it takes plenty of money to keep a home goin'."

"We've done our best," she murmured. "This old place is all we've got. And it's about to be taken from us."

"Mrs. Morrison, you don't have to tell me, but I'd like to hear about who's got their sights set on yer little home. I accept yer invitation to stay fer supper, only if you'll let me pay. From what you've told me, I'd say yer in no position to be handin' out charity."

"Maybe I'm not," she said, smiling wanly, "but I can't take your money for a meal's victuals. It wouldn't be a Christian act."

"All right, all right," he muttered. "It's not to my likin', though, to be takin' bread outta the mouths of fatherless children. I'm a real-estate man, Mrs. Morrison, I ain't sunk that low."

"I'm sure you haven't," she said with a smile.

When he took a good look at Ellie Morrison, his heart leapt. She was a handsome woman. Beautifully tall, and her figure was well-rounded in the way that men appreciate. Her features were lovely, too. Big brown eyes looked out of an oval-shaped face that was framed by hair as dark as midnight. Only the random gray strand betrayed the fact that she was no longer a girl in years, but a mature and beautiful woman. One who had suffered a grievous loss and who still bore the sorrow of that of loss.

The food she sat before him was plain fare, but Seth could not remember when he had enjoyed a meal more. The children occupied a bench at the back of the table. After they had eaten, they hurriedly left the kitchen to go back to playing in the yard.

Seth was glad they'd hurried away because he wanted to talk to their mother without them hanging on his every word. "Now, Mrs. Morrison," he said, "I don't mean to pry. But if you would, I'd like to hear more about this deal that's threatenin' yer home."

"There's nothing much to tell," she said. "After Ted got killed, I had to bury him decent-like, but I had no money to do it. So I had to mortgage the old place. My trouble is that I've not been able to repay the money. Now they say they're going to foreclose. Looks like me and the kids will be thrown out on the road. I don't know where we'll go, but if worse comes to worse, I'll do my best to keep us together."

"You ain't lost yer home yet," Seth said reflectively. "Tell me now, who holds the lien on yer property, an' how much is it fer?"

"The Mooney Bank in Woodsfield holds the mortgage. It's for five hundred dollars. The interest is overdue too. I haven't been able to repay anything since I got the money for my husband's funeral. It's about all I can do to feed Billy and Sue, and myself. I raise all the garden stuff I can, and then I can up what I can scrape together. We make out, or have so far. My only income, moneywise, is from some housework I get to do occasionally."

"I understand," he said, clearing his throat of a lump that had suddenly come into it. "I know them Mooney brothers. They're a grabbing lot of slickers. Give me all the details of yer loan an' perhaps I'll drop in on them one day next week. There ain't no love lost 'twixt me an' that bunch, so I won't worry none about bein' too rough on them."

As they talked, Ellie Morrison cleared the dishes from the table. Seth could feel his blood boiling in his veins like liquid fire as he watched her every graceful movement. Her dress was plain and worn almost to tatters, but it did not detract, in any way, from the attractiveness of her beautiful body. As she turned, and bent, and swayed, while clearing the table, her dress clung to her and showed in sharp relief every shapely contour of her lovely figure. He feasted his eyes upon her, unashamed of his desire and hunger.

When she bent over the table, he had a clear view down her dress of her full, rounded breasts. She wore no brassiere.

He inhaled sharply and she looked up, straight into his probing eyes. Brows knit in confusion, she looked down and realized the position she was in. A wave of red suffused her lovely features. Dropping her eyes, she sank into a chair.

"I'm-I'm sorry, ma'am," Seth said, trying as best he could to apologize for his rudeness. "So help me, I meant no offense." He stood up. "Reckon I better be on my way. Seems like I've wore out my welcome, even before it started."

"I accept your apology, Mr. Henderson," she said quickly, following him to the door and out onto the porch. "But don't go away feeling like that. Let's forget it ever happened. If you see them men at the bank in Woodsfield and don't come back, how will I know what they said about my home and the mortgage hanging over it?"

"I intended to come by again an' tell you. Perhaps it'd be better if I didn't, though. It wouldn't be right to pester you anymore after the way I insulted you just now."

"Oh, please, come and tell me," she implored.

"But, ma'am, maybe I wouldn't be welcome after the way I looked at you there in the kitchen. I meant you no harm, but I'm a man. I'm older than you by several years, but right now I don't feel that way. You're a sweet, beautiful, desirable woman, Ellie Morrison. Forgive me fer sayin' this to you after all you've told me about yer troubles, but I just had to."

"I understand, Mr. Henderson," she murmured, staring at him with her big expressive eyes. "Of course you're a man. But I believe you're a gentlemen, as well. I entreat you to come again and tell me what the Mooney brothers say about my indebtedness. Good-bye."

Bowing in farewell, Seth stepped off the porch, untied his horse, climbed up into his buggy, and drove away with his head whirling like a

school boy's. Ellie Morrison, even in their short acquaintance, affected him more than any of the beautiful wantons he had associated with on his trip down river. He laughed.

He felt positive that this lovely widow could love a man with all the fire of a tigress. She would not be like one of those painted and perfumed prostitutes that had disgusted him so. Yes, he admitted to himself, Ellie Morrison was indeed a woman. All woman.

"An', by heaven, I intend to have her," he growled, staring into the fiery summer sunset.

Thus it came about, that by taking a wrong turn on a strange road, a lonely widow came into his life . . . and was destined, thereafter, to give it meaning.

Chapter 4

The following Monday, Seth went to the Mooney Bank in Woodsfield, Ohio, and, after a heated session in the office of the bank statement president, purchased the note overshadowing the Widow Morrison's home.

"Listen, mister," Seth said, shaking a huge fist under the man's nose. "Keep yer big mouth shut. Moore ain't in on this deal. If you blab to him, I'll come back, an' you might find yer teeth growin' outta the back of yer neck. Understand?"

"Perfectly," the banker replied, smiling thinly. "What the papers do, however, is out of my hands. Local real-estate transactions are always printed, you know."

"I'm dependin' on you to keep it outta their hands," Seth growled. He stalked out of the office, slamming the door behind him.

For the next few days, Seth checked the *Woodsfield News* like clockwork. But no real-estate transactions, by him alone, were listed. On the following Saturday, he drove to Perkins Run and looked the old Murdock place over with a keen scrutiny, calculating its commercial potentialities. When he was satisfied with his survey, he wheeled his buggy up the narrow old road that led past the Widow Morrison's. As soon as he came in sight of the picturesque little home, his heart began pounding like the muffled boom of thunder.

He wasn't seriously interested in the Murdock farm, now that he'd seen it, but he intended to use it as an excuse to call on Ellie as long as he could get away with it.

When he drove up and alighted from his buggy, she came running out onto the porch, her beautiful face shining with genuine pleasure at his presence.

"Howdy, Ellie," he said with a grin, looking deep into her eloquent eyes. "It's me again. How come yer not carryin' a shotgun?"

"Hello, Mr. Henderson," she said, smiling in welcome. At his keen-eyed look, she blushed. "Now don't be silly. I haven't had a gun around the house since my husband's death. Please come up on the porch and sit down. I'm just dying to hear how you made out with that stingy banker. You did go to see him, didn't you?"

As he entered the yard, her little boy and girl interrupted their game of tag to give him questioning looks. Then almost immediately, they resumed their game.

Seating himself on the porch swing, Seth looked at the beautiful widow beside him and nodded his head gravely.

"Yep," he said. "I went to see that banker feller, but I ain't goin' to tell you a single thing that happened unless you agree to something first."

"What?" she asked, giving him a wide-eyed look filled with fear, suspicion, and mistrust. Seth burst out laughing. He understood. He was a strange man who had just made a request of her, a widowed woman with two kids to protect.

"Don't look so shocked," he said, chuckling. "I'm not goin' to ask you to sign yer life away. Nothin' as bad as all that. What I'd like is this: I want us to be friends. Very good friends. But we can't be if you insist on callin' me Mr. Henderson. From now on, that mister stuff has got to stop between us. I want to be just Seth to you, and you to be Ellie to me. Is that agreeable with you?"

"All right," she whispered, averting her gaze, but not before he had seen a mysterious light of gladness in her expressive eyes.

"Now, please, tell me," she begged. "Is the bank going to take my home away?"

"No, Ellie," he said. "Mooney ain't goin' to bother yer home, now or ever. I seen to that."

"I don't understand," she cried, looking at him in wonderment. "Please explain it to me . . . Seth."

"I can't, an' won't try to, right now. But take my word fer it. Yer home is safe."

As the afternoon progressed into evening, she tried, as is a woman's way, to learn what happened at the bank in Woodsfield concerning her home. Seth enjoyed the sweet and coy manner she employed to try to wheedle the information from him. But when he left at sunset, he was still in possession of his secret. He departed with her plea to come again ringing in his ears.

Over the next thirty days he visited the little house on the lonely ridge five times. Between visits, he stopped at the courthouse in Woodsfield and transferred her name to the paid note for her house; he even paid the taxes on the property so they were up to date. Her home was free of all debt.

Seth began to notice a gradual change in her attitude toward him. On his fourth visit, however, she seemed to be fighting a battle with herself, so she was moody and downcast. But on his fifth visit, she again expressed genuine gladness for his company. After supper, they sat in the swing, rocking back and forth. Seth took a deep breath and unburdened his heart.

"Look, Ellie," he said hoarsely. "I know I can't offer what I'd like to right now, but I love you. I love you so much I can't think straight anymore, or hold my tongue any longer. Be mine, darling. Mine all the way. I want so very, very much to utterly possess every sweet inch of yer body and cover it with kisses—from head to toe. An' while I'm doin' that, I want to be makin' love to you something horrible. Look at me, woman. Don't you hear a damn word I'm sayin'?"

"Yes, yes," she gasped, covering her crimson face with shaking hands. "Oh, Seth. I'm awfully fond of you. Please believe that I am. But I can't bring myself to do as you ask."

"Why not?" he demanded. "Yer a woman, ain't you? You know you need me just as much as I need you. Let's face the facts. I ain't slept with my wife fer three years or more. She's like a dead fish in bed. An' on top of that she hates my guts. Yer husband is dead, an' my wife is the same as dead, far as I'm concerned. So let's live a little, Ellie darling. Live while we're still alive an' able to still enjoy what we can give each other."

"No, no," she whispered. "I'll never give myself to any man out of wedlock. That would be adultery, Seth. To have sexual relations with you in our current situation would make me no better than a whore. Have you no respect for a poor widow and her fatherless children?"

"I love you, Ellie," he said again. "That's all I know. An' if loving you an' wantin' you like I do seems disrespectful, I'm sorry."

"Forgive me for saying what I did," she pleaded. "I know how you feel about me and the children. It shows in your every word and action. But surely you can understand my position."

"Position? Hell," he growled. "Right or wrong, Ellie darling, it's like I said before. I want to utterly possess that sweet, wonderful body of yours. That's how I feel. I know I can't marry you now; but if God's listenin' to me tonight, he'll know I speak truth when I say I will marry you just as soon as he releases me from the hell my life's become. Until that day, Ellie darling, let me love you all the way. Please believe in me."

"I can't, I can't," she cried brokenly. "For right now, let's just go on being friends. Surely that will be enough. If I can't give in to you like you want, I know you're too much of a gentleman to force a woman against her will."

"Aw, hell, Ellie," he groaned. "I'm not *that* much of a gentleman. I couldn't be even if my life depended on it. So stop this askin' me to soft pedal with you. I just can't, honey. It's got to be all the way with me—or nothin'. I'd go mad bein' around you, not bein' able to make love to you like I want. After all, I'm only flesh and blood, not stone."

"I know, I know," she whispered. "But what you're asking can't ever be between us."

"All right, then," he said wearily. "Reckon I better be on my way. Walk to the buggy with me. I'll say good-bye to you there."

After he untied his horse, he stood with her at the gate and waited, hoping she would make some sign that it would be acceptable for him to kiss her good night. But no such sign was forthcoming. Instead, she held out her hands and smiled up at him in the mysterious, provocative way that belongs to women alone. With a wry look, he clasped her proffered hands and looked down into her upturned face, his heart in his eyes.

"Good night, Seth," she murmured. "I must confess that I love you, too. But I honestly think I would hate myself, and you, if I let our relationship sink to the level of a back-street love affair."

"As I said before, Ellie, I only know the fire of my love for you. It's burning my insides out."

"I'm sorry, truly sorry," she whispered tremulously. "But what can I say, except—good night."

As she smiled up at him there in the summer moonlight, Seth threw caution to the wind and gathered her close to his breast, his hungry arms holding her in a vice-like grip. With a brutal passion, he claimed her soft upturned mouth in kiss after kiss.

When he released her, she stumbled back. Bowing her head, she burst into tears. He immediately tried to console her, but she fought back like a tigress, striking him with stinging blow after stinging blow in the face.

"Go," she sobbed. "You're no better than any of the other lowlifes I've been fighting off since Ted got killed. And I thought you was a gentleman! I believed you respected me."

"Ellie, Ellie," he pleaded. "I meant you no offense. I only—"

"Get out of my sight," she cried miserably.

"I'll go," he said in defeat. Then he reached into the buggy and drew forth a heavy manila envelope. "Guess you better take this, now that I won't be seein' you again," he said, handing it to her. "Just remember one thing when I'm gone. I love you, an' I always will. Good-bye."

Then he climbed aboard his buggy and drove away, leaving the sobbing widow standing in the road, looking wonderingly at the envelope she held in her hands.

■■■

The following twenty-one days were the longest Seth Henderson ever lived. During his waking hours, he fought a raging battle with himself.

Every fiber in his body told him to visit Ellie Morrison, just one more time, while his head said no.

At night, he would toss and turn in his lonely bedroom as she haunted his dreams.

He could see her sweet face and grief-filled eyes in the sunrise and sunset of every day. Even the clouds in the sky reflected her image into his sad eyes. Seth was hopelessly in love.

On the twenty-second day of his exile from the woman he loved, his wife, Amy, denounced him bitterly as a money-grubber and cheat. This was not the first time she had spoken to him in this manner since they had become estranged, but on this particular day, her biting scorn seemed to stab him through and through like a poisonous barb.

Unable to bear her company any longer, he grabbed his coat and hat and dashed out of the house.

He harnessed his driving mare, hitched her to the buggy, and drove off, uncaring of the direction he went. After hours of aimless driving, on roads he paid little attention to, he noticed a familiar ridgeline and realized he was on Perkins Run.

By now the day was far spent. In fact, the shades of night were already shutting in the valley. To the west, the evening star sparkled in the cloudless sky like a huge diamond.

Reining in his horse, Seth turned to stare in the direction of Ellie Morrison's home. A storm raged inside his chest. Minutes passed. At last, bowing to the inevitable, he clucked to his horse and drove on, away from Ellie.

"It'll be dark in a few minutes," he muttered. "What the hell. Don't reckon it'd do any harm to drive past the cabin. She'll be in bed by then an' will never know I went by. But oh God above, how I want to see her just once more." Resolved, he turned his horse around in a wide spot in the road and started down the valley. When he turned down the narrow dirt road that led past Ellie Morrison's, his blood sped up in his veins and his heartbeat commenced its muffled thunder in his ears.

As the little cabin came into sight, he thought his heart would burst in two. Wetting his dry lips, he slowed his horse to a walk.

The log cabin stood dark and silent, not a single light shone from within. And the only light from without was the light from the rising moon touching its shingled roof.

As he drove up alongside the yard gate, the horse stopped from force of habit. Seth sat and stared at the cabin with his heart in his eyes. Without knowing why, he climbed out of the buggy and tied the reins to the gate post. He stepped inside the yard and stopped. Removing his hat, he stood there a moment, staring at the cabin with aching eyes and heart. Sighing, he bowed his head and slowly walked back toward the road. After untying

his horse, he set a foot on the iron step of the buggy and began to draw himself up into the seat.

Sobbing arrested his movement. Spinning around, he looked at the cabin again. A human figure came dashing down the steps toward him. It was Ellie Morrison.

"Oh, Seth. Seth," she sobbed, flinging herself into his arms. "Thank God it's you. Oh, my darling, I thought you'd never come back."

"I'm here, honey, I'm here," he said. "I couldn't stay away. Believe me, I tried. But I couldn't. You said you hated me, an' I came anyway."

"I don't hate you, Seth Henderson," she whispered against his hungry mouth. "Don't you know by now that I love you? Love you regardless of all the promises I made to myself that I would never let it happen."

Sweeping her up into his arms, he walked to the porch and sat down with her on his lap. Then he loosed all the pent-up hunger and longing he had felt for her since the first day of their acquaintance. He covered her upturned face, her eyes, her cheeks, her throat, her lips with kisses. And she returned him kiss for kiss.

"Why did you do it, darling?" she asked as he kissed her throat. "It wasn't your debt. And all that gold in the envelope, too. Do you really love me so much?"

"Hush, my dearest," he said. "I cleared your home of debt because in my heart I look upon you as mine. I gave you the gold because I knew you needed it desperately, an' even though you held me off at arm's length, I knew I had to take care of you. I love you, Ellie Morrison. That's the way I feel about you."

"I know, I know," she whispered, reaching up and pulling his face down to hers, claiming his lips with her demanding ones.

Holding her tighter in his arms, Seth stood up and strode across the porch and into the cabin. Feeling his way with his feet, he found the bed in the corner. Placing Ellie on it, he turned and shut the cabin door. He walked back over to the bed and sat down on the edge of it. Ellie swung her feet over the side and put her arms around him. He began unbuttoning her dress.

"Oh, Seth. Seth," she whispered, a sob tearing at her throat. "Must we do it? Must we?"

"Yes, Ellie darling, we must," he said fiercely. "I've tortured myself near outta my mind from wantin' you. Tonight you are goin' to satisfy that hunger."

"Please, oh please," she pleaded. "Not here, if you must. Ted and me shared this bed. I was his *wife*; you and I aren't even engaged. We can't be because you're married. Oh, can't you see? Can't you understand how I feel about all this? If you just got to make me do it, let's go out and lay on the porch. Just not here on this bed."

"Hush, Ellie baby," he said softly between kisses on her protesting lips. "I understand. But you are gonna give yourself to me right here on this bed. Not outside on the cold porch. Ted's gone, honey. Gone forever. I'm sure he'd understand if you was dead an' he wanted another woman like I want you. Stop livin' in the past. Live fer you an' me an' Billy an' Sue. Live now, an' from now on."

He continued to undress her, and she continued to protest. But as he removed her garments one by one, her protests became weaker and weaker. Soon the only thing she had on was her panties.

Then Seth began to quickly disrobe. Once nude, he lay down beside her curled up form. She was sobbing softly. Pulling her into his arms, he kissed her lips and began caressing her. When he touched her full breasts, she trembled.

Against her low moaning protests, he slipped her panties off. When he put his hand between her legs, she fought to push it away. But Seth knew that victory was his, so he was patient and gentle.

While she struggled in vain to get away from him, he succeeded in obtaining the position he knew would turn the tide of her protests in his favor. An instant later she gasped and clutched at him with trembling hands, still softly moaning her protests.

As he moved his body on hers, she began breathing in fitful gasps, her breath thick and hot. For every movement he made, she gave a trembling squirm.

"Oh, darling, darling," she soon began to plead in a whisper. "I can't hold myself any longer. Go faster. Oh please, go faster. I'll just die dead if you don't. It's been so long since I've felt this way. I don't care if it hurts a little bit. Please, *please* don't slow down. Not now, not now. I'm about to—ahaaaaaa."

Her breath caught in her throat. In a gasping whisper, she told him she was having her orgasm. Then nature began exerting itself on Seth. With a few rapid thrusts, he reached his own completion and sank down into her arms, completely spent, completely satisfied, and completely happy. She kissed him, again, and again, with lips that were as sweet as wine.

Between kisses she whispered her love for him. Wordlessly happy, he clung to her and returned her caress, for caress.

The hours wore away. But to the lovers in the little cabin they passed like minutes. Ellie had surrendered all the way. Her former reserve and objections were forgotten like they had never been voiced.

In the cool gray light of the early dawn, he kissed her good-bye and took his departure, but not before he had claimed his love twice more. The fires of her passion, once roused, seemed unquenchable.

Thus did Seth Henderson succumb to the malady that has enslaved all men, especially husbands, since the beginning of time. Namely, the love of a strange woman.

Chapter 5

The next twelve years were the happiest ones Seth Henderson was to experience in his entire lifetime. After her first total surrender to his desires, Ellie Morrison fought against becoming his mistress with all the doubts, and fears, and tears, and religious objections that are the natural defense of a morally upright woman.

Nevertheless, Seth was adamant in his stand.

"I love you, Ellie," he would tell her every time she looked at him reproachfully before having sexual relations. "Can't you understand that an' stop torturing yourself—an' me. I promise we'll be married just as soon as Amy passes on. She's old an' sick an' about as pleasant to be around as a bear with a sore ass. An' besides that, she hates my guts. I can't divorce her. Bein' a woman, you outta know that. She'd see me dead an' in hell before she'd set me free to wed another woman. Let's face it, honey. Fer the present, I'm stuck with her."

But Ellie always asked the same question every time Seth came to her after being at the Henderson homestead. "Have you asked your wife for a divorce yet?" And at the admission that he had not, she never failed to advance numerous reasons why divorce, even with all its unpleasant repercussions, was far more honorable than the degrading situation existing between them.

At such times, Seth would take her into his arms, completely disregarding her objections, and kiss her lips and caress her in certain intimate places until her protests were stilled. More often than not, her response was so intense that he was hard put to satisfy her passionate demands. Even so, Ellie never criticized or belittled him. Instead, she was endearing and understanding. She possessed qualities that so many men search in vain for in their sweethearts and wives.

Six months after she became his woman, Seth bought an attractive house in Woodsfield and moved her and her children into it. This, however, was accomplished only after he'd repeatedly pointed out the advantages that such a move could give her.

After he'd moved her into town, Seth started spending one night a week with her. But always against her wishes. As time went by, he increased the frequency of his overnight stays. By the time another six months had passed, they were living together as man and "wife."

Her objections over their unholy relationship became more and more infrequent. And it wasn't long after they stopped that she began meeting him at the door every evening with clinging arms and eager lips. Most nights he welcomed these greetings with enthusiasm after being at the office all day. But some nights he was overly tired. On these nights, she would greet him with a kiss that was intimacy itself. Then she would wait on him hand and foot. First she would feed him a delicious meal, and then she would gently bathe him. And while she bathed him, she would whisper compliments in his ears about his body, paying particular attention to his generous manhood.

Once they were in bed, she would cuddle and fondle him in a way that was hers alone. He would quickly forget his tiredness and make unbridled love to her. And when they reached their climaxes, she would lay limply in his arms completely satisfied, her breaths coming in gasps and her body all sweaty and she-smelling.

Seth found it endearing, for while Ellie possessed the passionate intensity of a tigress during their moments of lovemaking and always gave generously of herself, she always kept herself as meticulously groomed as possible. To see her otherwise, because of him, made him happy.

···

After he began making his home with Ellie, it was not unusual for Billy and Sue to sit at his feet and beg him to tell them stories of his boyhood. They had taken to Seth right from the start. In return, he loved them and tried his best to fill the void left in their lives at the loss of their father. His relationship with his own sons, however, was not as good.

In the fifth year of his residence with Ellie, his sons Silas and George married and moved to a branch of Duck Creek, twenty miles away. Later that same year, Charles, his eldest, met him in the square in Woodsfield and refused the hand Seth extended to him.

"Seth," he said bitterly, "I can't look on you as my father any longer after what happened to me last week."

"I don't understand, son," Seth muttered. "Why not tell me about it. Maybe I can help."

"You can, but you won't" was Charles's biting retort.

"Try me an' see."

"All right, if you're interested in helping me, here it is: Give up this foolishness you've got goin' on with that woman and come back to Mother."

"Son, you don't know what yer askin'," Seth growled. "What has my comin' back to yer mother got to do with you?"

"Everything" was his grim reply.

"How so?"

"You remember Ruth Thomas?"

"Reckon I know who you mean. Does her folks live over in Straight Fork, below Graysville?"

"That's right. Anyway, her and me have been engaged for over three months. Then last week— right outta a clear sky—she broke off with me. And it's all your fault."

"Go on."

"Seems like her mother found out about you living with another woman here in Woodsfield. That sure cooked my goose with Ruth."

"I'm listenin'," Seth growled. "Tell me the rest."

"She claimed her mother would never let a daughter of hers marry any feller whose father is, she said, 'shacking up with a cheap hussy.' That was her words. I begged her to change her mind, but she said she agreed with her mother a hundred percent. Now you know the spot your horsing around has put me in."

Seth's face turned red with rage.

"Listen, Charley," he said, clenching his fists. "There's always two sides to every story, an' that's the case in mine. Any girl who'd condemn a boy just because of his father's shortcomings ain't worth a pinch of snuff. Go tell this split-tail as much—an' make sure that long-nosed mother of hers hears it too."

"I can't, Dad," Charles said stubbornly.

"I don't see why not. I say tell 'em. An' if they don't like what they hear, to hell with 'em. A man's got to stand on his own two feet in this life, son. The quicker you learn that, the happier you'll be."

"But I feel that Ruth and her mother are right. Look, Dad, be reasonable. This deal you've handed Mother and us boys looks bad. And you know it."

"Charley, there's things between yer mother an' me you boys don't know about."

"Like what?" Charles demanded.

"Yer mother shut me outta her life long before I quit comin' home."

"I don't believe you," Charles snapped.

"Well, it's the gospel truth," Seth said. "An' another thing, yer mother locked me outta her bedroom. You're not married yet, so you can't imagine what a thing like that can do to a man's self-respect."

"Poppycock. Sex ain't that important to a man your age."

"Sex is important to every man, of every age," Seth replied grimly. "Pick out any old-timer an' ask him. You don't have to take my word for it."

"You mean to say this woman you're shacking up with can give you something my mother can't?" young Charles Henderson asked in a strained voice.

"It's true, Charley," Seth said. "To start with, yer mother hates me. She's hated me fer years. But this 'hussy,' as you called her, I'm shacked up with loves me. An' I love her. I love her like I once loved yer mother, before she turned her back on me. I'm sorry things has got to be this way between me an' my family, but I can't help it."

"Dad, for the last time, I'm askin' you to give up this woman and come home. You and Mother can still find happiness. At least give it a try."

"I can't," Seth said stubbornly. "I love Ellie Morrison, an' she loves an' respects me. That's more than I can say fer yer mother."

"What about Ruth an' me?" Charles asked, his face ashen. "What about our happiness?"

"You two young people will have to work out yer own differences. Yer a *man*, an' she's a woman. Stand on yer own feet, son. That's the best advice I can give you."

"And you refuse to come back to Mother?"

"I do," Seth said quietly.

"All right," Charles Henderson said, his face livid with the rage of a boy who feels his father has deeply wronged and shamed him. "I should've known you hadn't the backbone to give this woman up. So keep right on stayin' with your whore. To hell with both of you."

Turning on his heel, Charles Henderson stalked away, blind to the crowd of curious onlookers who had gathered at the first sound of heated words between father and son. Bowing his head, Seth left as quickly as possible. Strangers listening to his family troubles was the last thing he desired.

He didn't mention the encounter with his son to Ellie. Deeply religious woman that she was, she would have blamed herself for the rift between him and his family. And that, he could never let her do.

"Let 'em stew in their own juices," he muttered as reviewed the whole matter in his head in the days that followed. "They kicked me outta their lives years ago. Now let 'em work out their own problems. I'm not gonna

listen when they come whinin' to me because things have snapped back in their faces. I wouldn't give one of Ellie's little fingers fer the lot of 'em."

...

A few months after meeting with his son, Seth's business partner, James Moore, found out about his relationship with Ellie Morrison. And, as is the way of some narrow-minded men, tried to cut himself in on what he considered a juicy setup.

"Look, partner," Moore said one day at the office. "Let's face it. You ain't the man you once was, regardless of how you feel about it. Old Father Time does things to even the best of us."

"So?"

"Well, yesterday on the street, I met the woman that you're shacked-up with. She's sure some looker. And what a shape."

"What're you tryin' to say?" Seth asked mildly, pretending that Moore's words weren't making his blood boil.

"Simply this," Moore replied, smiling nastily. "This babe is just too much woman for an old duffer like you. So, wise up."

"Keep talkin'."

"Why not cut me in on this deal? I'm a much younger man than you, and I've got more on the ball. I could keep the wire-edge jazzed off her. That way you could coast along and take it easy. Actually, I'd be doing you a favor."

"What makes you think that I can't take care of her bedroom needs, as you put it?" Seth asked. He wanted to feel his partner out before putting him in his place once and for all.

"Hell, Seth," Moore said, laughing. "Let's not play games with each other. I'm willing to bet the last dime I'll ever have that that sexy bitch has still got enough fire left in that little spot between them pretty legs of hers to take care of the needs of ten ordinary men, let alone one old workhorse like you."

"What are you sayin'?"

"Take me home with you tonight. That way I could get started with her before you're so fagged-out, you start talking to yourself. Play it smart. She's got plenty of zip for both of us. And anyway, we're partners, ain't we? Share and share alike."

With a roar like that of an angry lion, Seth lunged across the desk separating them and yanked his partner clean out of his chair. Holding the man at arm's length, Seth shook a clenched fist in his partner's terror-stricken face.

"Listen, you slimy rat, an' listen well," he snarled. "I'm only tellin' you this once, so you better pay heed to what I'm sayin'. I live with Ellie Morrison because I love her an' her kids. She loves me too. What quilt-

fightin' we can give each other is only part of our relationship. She's the finest; kindest; most wonderful woman I've ever known. But I don't expect the likes of you to understand a thing like that."

"Easy, Seth, old man," Moore said, squirming around like a mouse caught in a trap. "I meant no harm to this woman of yours. I apologize."

"Yer damn well right you better not have," Seth growled, flinging Moore back into his chair. "If you so much as lay one of yer dirty looks on Ellie, I'll fracture yer skull. You an' me are in business together to make money. There'll be no monkey business in each other's private lives on the side. Get me?"

"Sure, sure," Moore said quickly. "Only for heaven's sake get hold of yourself, man. Keep this woman all to yourself. More power to you.

There's no need for you to blow your stack the way you just did. No female's worth it."

"See that you keep feelin' that way . . . partner," Seth said, smiling mirthlessly. "Otherwise, we're liable to tangle. AN' I DO MEAN TANGLE."

Thereafter, Seth never relaxed his guard around Moore. He had never exactly trusted the man, and now that Moore had openly voiced his interest in Ellie, Seth trusted him even less. In turn, Moore made it abundantly clear that he now hated Seth.

Seth had learned from hard experience that once a snake, always a snake. Consequently, he began to sharply curtail all deals with Moore, taking no chances that Moore would wipe him out financially through some shrewd business juggling.

James Moore, however, would not be the one to bring Seth Henderson down. No, fate was ready to play another trump card in the life of Seth Henderson.

···

In April of 1917 the United States became involved in a European conflict that had been raging overseas for almost three years.

Thirteen months later, an epidemic of influenza struck in the United

States. It soon assumed pandemic proportions and swept the nation. At that time, the infection was comparatively mild, with few complications and many recoveries.

The second wave of the disease occurred six months later. This time it was fatal.

Doctors were powerless to cope with the virus and people began dying by the thousands. In Woodsfield, Ohio, Ellie Morrison was one of its earliest victims.

One day she was in the best of health, and the next day she was burning up with fever. Seth immediately cancelled all his business at the

office to concentrate on nursing her back to health. But the sting of death had already touched the woman he loved.

For three days after her fever broke, she lay wan and still, with hardly a sign of life about her. On the fourth day, she rallied and, smiling at Seth and her children, asked for her Bible.

At her whispered request, Seth felt as though an icy hand was clutching his heart. With an encouraging word and a cheery smile, he handed her the well-worn book she had brought with her from the little cabin above Perkins Run.

At intervals during the rest of the day, she read the Good Book. Sometimes her lips would even move while her eyes were closed. When Seth saw this, he knew she was praying, and his heart became a leaden weight inside his breast.

That night as he dozed by her side, she slipped away. Neither a whisper nor a cry marked her passing. When he awoke hours later, the hand he held was rigid and cold in death.

He buried Ellie beside her husband, Ted, in a small unkempt cemetery on a lonely ridge that was not far from where he had first met her twelve years before. As he stood by the open grave that bleak November day, snow falling all around, he felt as though they were also burying his heart in that hole in the ground.

Shortly afterward, Seth had a handsome headstone erected over the graves. He had her name and her husband's inscribed on it with the dates of their births and deaths. The following month he arranged for Billy and Sue to make their home, from then on, with Ellie's married, childless sister in Pittsburgh. He loved the children, so before he bade them good-bye, he deposited a goodly amount of money to their credit in a Pittsburgh bank with instructions that it be used, exclusively, to pay for their upbringing and education.

After the loss of the woman he loved, Seth gradually reverted back to his gold-hungry self of other days. The United States settled hostilities with the European aggressor, and for the next five years, Seth and Moore rode the gravy train in the real-estate boom of the post-war years. He still mistrusted his business partner, so shortly after his seventy-second birthday, he severed all connections with the man and went into retirement.

"I've worked enough," he told himself the day he retired from active dealing. "From now on, I'm takin' it easy. Reckon I better, 'cause I'm livin' on borrowed time."

After Ellie Morrison's death, Seth's wife and sons made numerous overtures of reconciliation. But his heart was sore inside him, and he always turned a deaf ear to all their entreaties. Nevertheless, God Almighty had other plans for the hard-shelled old farmer.

Each winter since the great pandemic of influenza in 1918 and 1919, the disease always returned. It was not as severe by 1923, but it still claimed an appalling number of lives through the help of its time-tested accomplice—pneumonia.

In November of that year, the year of his retirement, Seth fell victim to this tenacious virus. Since he was living alone, the doctor immediately notified his family to help take care of him.

As soon as he had sufficiently recovered, Seth's sons took him back to the Henderson homestead, a tired, broken old man. Before he would consent to return with them, though, he purchased a huge iron safe and placed all his gold and records inside it, keeping the combination a secret from every member of his family.

Once back on the farm, he went through the motions of living, his zest for life having been buried in a lonely grave, on a lonely ridge, miles away.

But time heals all scars, and so it was with Seth Henderson. His son Charles had won out over his girlfriend's objections to marrying him, so by the time Seth came back to his old home, two bright-faced grandchildren were there to greet him. Before the winter was over, they had won the heart of their crusty, mistrusting grandfather.

In late April of 1924, Seth was stricken again. It wasn't long before he was bedridden and so weak that he could hardly feed himself. It was obvious to him that his time on this earth was short.

"Bring me my gold," he instructed Charles one Sunday evening. He whispered the combination of the safe into Charles's ear when he bent close. When Charles placed the box of gold coins on the bed beside his emaciated form, Seth sat up and ran his fingers through the gold coins. Then he looked at his family clustered around his bed with an awful light shining in his eyes. All his sons and their families were at his bedside that evening. His wife, Amy, had celebrated her seventieth that day, and the family had gathered for the occasion. He looked at each family member in turn, as though trying to draw a measure of strength from their youthful presence.

With a strange choking cry, Seth flung the gold from him; then, gasping for breath, he fell back on the bed. In that moment Seth Henderson had come face to face with an appalling truth. That which had ruled his life for so long had become a canker on his soul. He was facing death, and he was terrified.

"Amy," he whispered, "help me. I'm dying, and I'm afraid to die. What can I do?"

"Pray to God," she said, smiling understandingly and taking hold of his shaking hands. "You've wandered away, but he'll welcome you into the fold. Pray now, before it's too late."

Clutching the time-worn hands of his silvery-haired wife, Seth poured out his fears to God in the manner of a frightened child. Earth and heaven were slipping away, and he knew he had no place to stand. God heard his supplication, and that night he slept soundly for the first time in weeks.

"Give my old neighbors the gold I cheated them out of years ago," he instructed his family the next day. "I might pass on anytime now, an' when

I go, I don't want that deal on my soul. Amy, please listen to me while I'm able to talk. I'm truly sorry for what happened between us in the past. If you hadn't shut me outta yer heart an' life, I probably wouldn't have strayed. Forgive me, an' don't think too badly of Ellie. She was a good woman. She didn't even—"

"Hush, husband of mine," Amy said soothingly. "I understand, so rest in peace. I was more wrong than you. I know that now. I bear no ill will toward Ellie Morrison. She was a woman in love. And no one has the right to condemn a person for loving. Only God can search out the good or bad in a heart."

The following week Seth Henderson closed his eyes forever. At long last he was in harmony with God and his fellowmen. Thus it was, that in death, the tired old farmer found the peace that had eluded him for so long in his life.

Retribution At Midnight

It was inevitable. In fact, there are those who would tell you that it was his way of life that eventually brought justice down on his head, this man who had always rode roughshod over everything and everybody. This man was Biff Daggett.

Biff was a lumberjack. Tall, broad, and straight as a jack pine; he could lick his weight in wildcats. Knowing his atrocious temper, every man and boy in Stumpville always gave him a wide berth whenever he was tanked up on "mountain dew." On such occasions, his raven hair would stand up like a lion's mane and he would be about as pleasant to tangle with as a buzz saw.

Another obnoxious characteristic of Biff's that did not endear him to the men of the community was his constant parading of himself as God's one gift to women. Consequently, he possessed the warped idea that every member of the opposite sex was fairly swooning for him to pay court to her. And therein lay his downfall.

Whenever a new girl of courting age moved into the neighborhood, not a single man or boy dared to make a move until Biff had first looked her over.

If she met with his approval, all others would respectfully stand aside and permit him, Beau Brommell Daggett, to squire the new girl around town to his heart's content, without the slightest interference from anyone.

Should any of the unmarried men, in a rash moment, overstep the limitations Biff had laid out for them, he would promptly administer black eyes and knocked-out teeth, uncaring of who received what.

This method of keeping the opposition in line had always worked marvelously for him. Until the fall of his twenty-fifth birthday. Then his tyrannical rule stuck a snag.

...

In early October the teacher of the grade school in Stumpville suddenly took ill. Being the frail type, her condition steadily grew worse. Finally, her doctor ordered her to take a long rest and suggested she avail herself of the sunshine and high dry air found in Southern California. When her resignation became final, the school was left without a teacher. A replacement was immediately sought.

The day Marcella Rand arrived in Stumpville to fill the position all hell broke loose among the men of the community—married and single alike.

Not only did this little lady possess an unusual beauty, but her figure would have put many a burlesque queen to shame. Her oval-shaped face with its gray-green eyes and even white teeth was framed by a halo of lustrous auburn hair that flowed in a rippling wave past her shoulders. Added to that, she had firm jutting breasts, a tiny waistline, shapely legs, and apple-round hips that wiggled and swayed most provocatively as she walked.

Considering her many, well-developed, physical charms, Miss Rand was, without question, a delectable package of femininity that men would commit mayhem over, even in church. And the current state of backwoods Stumpville was far from being peaceful and serene like the inside of a church.

As soon as Biff set eyes on the luscious Marcella, he issued a proclamation, to all and sundry, that the new schoolmarm was, but definitely, his own private dish.

"Hands off, you tomcats," he admonished his rivals, shaking his huge fists to emphasize his words. "Either that, or I'll put half of you under the care of Doc Adams. This little filly is just the babe yours truly has been pinin' fer. Give me a month or so with her an' we'll be waltzin' down the aisle, hand in hand."

But, as is the way of many a man's plans concerning a woman, things did not work out for Biff as he had anticipated.

···

Besides being a young woman of unusual beauty, Marcella Rand was also possessed of unusual levelheadedness. Consequently, she soon let it be known that she wanted no part of the coarse, unlettered Biff, or any of his uncouth companions.

This turndown, by the most beautiful girl the residents of Stumpville had ever seen, was a crushing blow to the ego of Beau Brommell Daggett. But, never being one to leave a challenge unchallenged, he quickly acquired some literature on social etiquette and painstakingly endeavored to transform himself into a man of ease and charm in any surrounding.

During the weeks that immediately followed his studies, he attended every social gathering Miss Rand did in hopes of impressing her with his newly learned skills.

It's sad that his efforts were all in vain. It was painful to watch the giant lumberjack at social gatherings. He made all kinds of unpardonable blunders, and he created a multitude of embarrassing situations, for himself and others. He would go bumbling through an evening's entertainment about as at home in his new-found environment as a bull in a china shop.

When Marcella publicly snubbed him several times on the main street of Stumpville—and before witnesses!—he threw in the sponge regarding the etiquette and straightaway reverted to his former tyrannical self.

"I'll show that high-browed heifer," he boasted, disregarding his companions' scornful laughter. "No painted-up street walker can cut Biff Daggett in public like she did an' git away with it. Mark my words, I'll show her a thing or two yet."

His companions, however, wasted scant sympathy on him and his injured pride. The rebuffs he had received from the beautiful schoolmarm were something they had longed for, for years. People do not easily forget the embarrassment and discomfort of black eyes and knocked-out teeth, especially when they are inflicted by an overbearing bully. And so it was with the less muscular gentry of Stumpville.

Then something happened that was to have a far-reaching effect on the life of Biff Daggett.

For more than ten years, the Interstate Lumber Company had operated a sizable mill in Stumpville. The payroll for the company's Stumpville employees had been complied in Grantsburg, then the paychecks had been shipped by rail upriver to Stumpville every payday. All this was about to change.

An accountant, and payroll computer, was being transferred to Stumpville to handle the company's books and employees' paychecks, and he was scheduled to arrive this week.

Percival Potts was his name, and, from a purely physical standpoint, he was the direct opposite of Biff Daggett. When the train ground to a wheezing, clanging stop that Saturday afternoon, Potts lurched off it . . . and almost fell. He was too busy wrestling with a huge steel suitcase, which was obviously far too heavy for him to handle, to watch where he stepped.

Dropping the suitcase onto the station platform, he drew himself up to his full five feet and timidly asked a group of belted and booted bystanders the whereabouts of the Interstate Lumber Company offices.

At his soft-voiced inquiry, a howl of pure enjoyment issued from the lounging lumberjacks, who had come down to the station to watch the evening train roll in.

"Well, if it ain't a dude," one said gleefully in disbelief. They all burst into gales of laughter.

Biff Daggett, being one of the bystanders, laughed loudest and longest of any.

"You the payroll figgerer?" he asked the diminutive stranger.

"I am."

"Yer name?" Biff persisted.

"Percival Potts" was the polite reply.

"Well, I'll be a pop-eyed son of a gun," Biff yelled gleefully, convulsing with laughter. "Feller, you take the cake. But with a handle like yer packin' it's not too surprisin'. This timber outfit sure must be gettin' hard up fer help to send a scrawny bird like you up here to do a man's job."

"The company offices, sir," Percival said again. "Could you please direct me to them?"

"With pleasure," Biff said with a grin. Then he spit a stream of tobacco juice from between his teeth. It hit the plank flooring of the station platform and splattered onto the polished shoes of Percival Potts. "The offices is right up that muddy road yer lookin' at. I'd go with you and show you the way, only it'd be too risky. I'd never live it down if the folks of this burg caught me nursemaidin' a pimp like you. Ha-ha."

As time passed, it soon became evident, especially to Biff Daggett, that Percival Potts was a man of hidden qualities. The new citizen of Stumpville was a neat dresser and well educated, and he conducted himself to good advantage at all the social gatherings he attended.

These accomplishments did not heighten Biff's estimation of the man, considering the spectacle he had made of himself but recently at similar social gatherings. Then when Marcella Rand began showing an interest in the studious accountant, his blood began to boil.

"See here, you pencil-pushin' runt," he growled, accosting Potts one day in mid-November when he chanced to meet him on the plank sidewalk of Stumpville's main street. "I'm givin' you fair, *fair* warnin'. Stay yer distance, as far as that snooty schoolmarm is concerned. She's goin' to share my bunk come green-up time, only she don't know it yet."

"I believe you're Daggett," Percival murmured, eyeing the fuming lumberjack mildly. "Glad to have made your acquaintance. Now if you'll excuse me—"

"Not so fast, Pottsy," Biff snarled, grabbing the front of Percival's business suit and yanking the smaller man up on his toes. "I'm addressin' you, feller. An' take it from yer uncle Biff—you *better* pay attention. Now, about that prissy chick yer nosin' around. She's rank pissin' fer you, see? What I mean, Pottsy, is that from here on in, long as she hangs her hat in this burg, she's mine. And don't you forget it."

"Mr. Daggett, I declare. Surely you can't be serious. Miss Rand and I are only very good friends at present, and nothing more."

"'Good friends,' my foot. In the future, you'll be usin' yer head to avoid her like the plague."

"Indeed, Mr. Daggett. As I see it, whom Miss Rand associates with is entirely up to her own discretion. Neither you nor I have any say in the matter."

"Says who," the irate lumberjack growled, shaking Percival like a terrier would a rat. "Fer your information wise guy, I'm the big frog in this here puddle. You'd best remember it. If Miss Snooty Rand wants a free hand in choosin' her gentlemen friends, she better pack up an' head outta Stumpville. She snubbed my offers of courtin'; an' in my book, that ain't no better than slappin' a man in the face. This is *my* burg. An' I'll be damned if I'm goin' to let a honky-tonk gal like her make a fool of me in it. Do I make myself clear?"

"Indubitably," Percival said. "But I still think you're abusing authority unwisely. Why not be a good fellow and forget any wrongs and slights you think you've received. It's the gentlemanly thing to do."

"Never," Biff roared, shaking the smaller man so hard that his hat flew off. When the expensive homburg landed at Biff's feet, the raging lumberjack gave it a violent kick that sent it sailing out into the muddy street. Releasing the squirming man, Biff swung his booted foot again. It connected with a thud against the seat of Percival Potts's pants. The man was thrust forward, out into the mud and mire, to land in a most undignified manner, within arm's reach of his hat.

"You've had yer warnin'," Biff said, glaring down at his fallen adversary. "Next time I'll do more than muss up yer duds an' skimmer. If you rile me much further, I'll break yer skinny neck like I would a dry stick. Stay away from my woman."

"When I need your advice, Mr. Daggett, I'll ask for it," Percival snapped as he picked himself up and began wiping the mud and filth off his clothes. He peered up at the towering lumberjack and, for a brief moment, a steely glint flared in his bespectacled eyes. But the look was lost on Biff.

His warning delivered, Biff turned away and stalked off down the street, his heavy hobnailed boots ringing hollowly on the wooden sidewalk.

Despite Biff Daggett's warning to the contrary, Percival Potts continued to pay court to the beautiful Marcella. And shortly after the birth of the New Year, they were married in the First Methodist Church in

Grantsburg.

Following a two-week honeymoon, Percival and his lovely bride moved into a reconditioned four-room bungalow that sat on a ten-acre plot of land a third of a mile up from Stumpville along the Little Kanawha River.

The new bride quickly transformed the little home into a paradise for the unassuming man she had chosen for her husband. Her handiwork soon became the envy of every other housewife for miles around.

She and Percival were very happy in their new home. And fortunately, both were able to retain the positions they had held prior to their marriage. Each weekday morning they would walk into Stumpville and resume their duties for the day. In the evening, they would meet at a prearranged spot and walk home together, hand in hand.

The citizens of Stumpville, and the surrounding community, accepted Marcella's marriage to Percival Potts as a matter that was strictly her own business. With typical rural openheartedness, they quickly conducted themselves as being happy in her happiness. But such was not the case with Biff Daggett.

The beautiful schoolteacher's rebuff to his advances had long been a sore spot upon his manly pride. And since her marriage to the diminutive Potts, that spot had grown and raged inside his breast until it had now assumed cancerous proportions. Nor did his companions help in any way to remedy his condition.

Every Saturday night the men of the woods would gather in Stumpville's only saloon to drink and make merry until the wee small hours of the Sabbath morn.

During these nights of revelry, they never failed to remind Biff that he was a has-been as far as the fairer sex was concerned.

Sometimes Biff would silence their malicious digs with a bull-like roar of rage and the menacing shake of his huge fists. At other times, he would endure their fiendish sport in glowering silence, getting drunker, and drunker, by the hour.

"Well now, Daggy, ol' hoss," one would jab at him. "Have ya set eyes on the schoolmarm lately?"

"Reckon he ain't," another would reply mournfully. "Leastwise not many times since she's become Mrs. Potts. But ain't that gal lookin' happy an' satisfied these days, though?"

"She sure is," a third would chime in. "But I guess there's only one sensible way to look at a thing like that. Our pencil-pushin' friend, that one that beat Daggy's time with her, must be some sort of expert when it comes to lovin'. Yes sirree, he sure must."

"It just couldn't be any other way," a fourth would observe sagely. "Wimmin, an' especially the butt-wigglin' kind like she is, wouldn't settle fer less than complete satisfaction in bed. You can't blame 'em much fer feelin' that way about it either. A gal with her looks an' figure can pick the best any day in the week. An' no foolin'. Too bad our pal Daggy didn't measure up to her requirements."

"You are so right. It's pitiful," a fifth would groan as though in great misery. "And that kind of puts all us timber fellers under a shameful cloud. But I got to hand it to that dude she hitched up with, bein' able to talk her into waltzin' down the aisle on his arm and all. Oh well, what the hell. Some fellers has what it takes to hook the wimmin they crave—and some don't. Eh, Daggy?"

"That's just the way it stacks up," another would insist loudly. "Boys, I take off my hat to this here Potts feller. He was the better man, an' he won. Now just take a squint at the clock there behind the bar. It stands at eleven thirty. In other words, bedtime fer all honest hardworkin' schoolmarms an' payroll figgerers. Why, I'd be plumb willin' to lay any one of you a month's wages, that right at this very minute, Mister Potts is up there in that shack putting our sweet little schoolmarm to bed. An' then I'll wager he's fixin' to crawl right in there beside her. Woo-wee. What wouldn't I give to trade places with him. How about you, Daggy? It's stormin' an' cold out tonight. Just right fer cuddlin' close an' lovemakin' .

. . country style. Ha-ha."

Thus it went almost every Saturday night. Consequently, Biff Daggett was fast reaching a point in his mind where he felt that violence against the man who had taken the lovely Marcella away from him was the only solution to quench the raging passion that churned within him.

One drizzly night in mid-April, after hours of guzzling rotgut whisky in the saloon, Biff lurched out of the place and soon found himself staggering up the river road that led to the Potts's bungalow.

When he partially regained his senses, he hesitated. Then he snapped his jaw shut and strode on, determined, at last, to give Percival Potts a taste of the violence that had been raging inside him for months.

"Damn yer yeller-bellied hide to hell, Potts," he muttered as he stalked on, making no effort whatsoever to sidestep the deep mud holes that pockmarked the road. "I'm goin' to knock you fer a row of backhouses tonight. Fer once, that tramp you hooked up with is goin' to have a real man to bed down with. Yes indeed."

When he came in sight of the residence he sought, he noted with satisfaction that a light was burning in the front room.

"Good," he growled, increasing his pace. "Git yer duds off, baby. This is sure my night to howl."

As he stalked into the yard, and then stomped up the porch steps, a dog of mixed breed came racing from around the bungalow and sprang at him with a snarl. With a well-aimed kick, Biff upended the canine so violently that it scurried for cover, yipping painfully.

Reaching the door, he banged on it loudly with a clenched fist. "Open up, dude," he bellowed. "I've come to spend the night."

"Who's there?" someone asked from inside. Biff instantly recognized the voice of Percival Potts.

"It's me. Biff Daggett," he replied loudly, giving the door a resounding kick with one of his heavy hobnailed boots. "Open up, damn you. Or I'll break this hen-skin door in."

"Go home, Daggett," Percival advised. "You're intoxicated, and we're not in any mood to entertain drunken visitors at this late hour. It's after midnight."

"The hell you say," Biff roared, giving the door another vicious kick. "When yours truly comes callin', he's always welcome—regardless of the hour. Now, you skinny bastard, OPEN THIS DOOR. Or I'm bustin' 'er down."

"Mr. Daggett, please be a good fellow and go home," Marcella pleaded in a quavering voice. Womanly intuition told her the reason for the lumberjack's drunken visit. "I just know you're too much of a man to go around disturbing people in the middle of the night. Now aren't you?"

By appealing to his manhood, she thought that she could dissuade him from any violence he intended to inflict on her husband.

"Guess again, you triflin' flirt" was Biff's snarling reply. "You wasn't too much of a lady to play fast and loose with my affections, then shake that round behind of yours in my face when you cut me cold. An' I ain't too much of a gentleman to call yer hand at that little game. Ha-ha."

"Daggett, you lie," Percival snapped indignantly, loyal, as all good husbands are, to the beautiful woman he had wooed and wed. "My wife made it very clear from the first day you met her that she wanted no part of you, or your bullying tactics. So I'm asking you again to clear out before there's trouble. Persist in this foolishness and I'll phone the constable in Stumpville. Maybe a few days in jail would teach you some sense."

Moving to the edge of the porch, Biff grabbed the telephone wire that ran from the party line into the bungalow, and with one powerful yank, he pulled it loose from the fuse box. The telephone was rendered useless. Percival Potts and his wife were now cut off from outside communication. Both were completely at his mercy. Or so Biff Daggett thought.

"Phone all the law this side of hell, Pottsy," he roared with glee. "In the meantime," he said, returning to the door, "I'm comin' in to do a bit of lovin' with Mrs. Potts. Ha-ha. We'll see whether this virgin beauty you hitched up with wants any part of yours truly or not. The truth is, after tonight, she'll want no more of yer halfway messin' around. After tonight, you'll be through in this shack, Pottsy."

Percival Potts tried in vain to argue the irate lumberjack out of his rapacious intentions. But his pleas fell on deaf ears. In desperation, the frightened payroll accountant disclosed that his bride of but three months was not well.

"What's wrong with our purty schoolmarm?" Biff murmured mockingly. "Got a sudden bellyache or somethin'?"

"My wife's going to have a baby," Percival said hoarsely.

The drunken lumberjack laughed in disbelief.

"That's a good one. Why, you skinny runt, I doubt if you're man enough to daddy a grasshopper, let alone git with a calf a hot-blooded babe like you're nestin' with. Mother Nature wouldn't insult us natives of Stumpville like that. No sirree, she sure wouldn't. But after I git through cuddlin' her tonight, I wouldn't want to lay you odds that she won't drop a calf in nine months. Unlock the door, Pottsy. 'Cause if you don't, I'm gonna break it down. I'm through arguin'."

"Never," Percival Potts said with the calmness of despair. "Break in here, Daggett, and one of us will get hurt. I warn you."

"You've no shootin' iron, so I ain't worried," Biff said smugly. Then he kicked out a panel in the upper part of the door. Thrusting his head into the opening, he laughed in fiendish glee at the sight of Percival and his lovely wife clinging to each other in terrible fear.

"Git outta that nightshirt, baby," he instructed the terror-stricken Marcella as a ghoulish smile parted his bearded lips.

"Git lost, runt," he said to the cowering Percival. "One more peep outta you, an' I'll twist yer scrawny neck. Me an' yer blushin' bride's got things to do. An' believe me, our plans sure don't include you. Ha-ha."

Reaching a hairy forearm through the opening in the door, Biff began fumbling with the key that was sticking in the lock.

Galvanized into action, Percival Potts gave a cry like that of an animal defending its mate to the death and grabbed a new hatchet lying on the center table. Swinging it aloft, he ran to the door.

The sight of that gleaming blade flashing over his head rendered Biff Daggett incapable of movement. And when he realized its deadly potential, action was too late.

Like a streak of light, Percival brought the hatchet whistling down. With a sickening, bone-cutting sound, the razor-sharp blade half-buried itself in Biff's upturned face.

A scream of mortal agony was wrenched from the lumberjack as he jerked his head out of the broken door and lurched off the porch, his life-blood spurting from his lacerated face.

Percival Potts made no effort whatsoever to succor his wounded enemy. Instead, he began administering to the needs of his pregnant wife, who had fallen to the floor in a dead faint.

...

During the months that immediately followed, the residents of Stumpville often commented on the sudden, and mysterious, disappearance of Biff Daggett from the local scene.

It was as though the very earth itself had opened up and swallowed him. No one in the community had seen neither hide nor hair of him since the night in April when Percival Potts had struck him with a hatchet in defense of his wife's honor.

After explaining what had happened to the constable, the man shook his grizzled head at the violence of youth and told Percival and his wife to think no more about it.

"Served Biff right" was the constable's quiet acceptance of the matter. "He's been tryin' to run things around here with too high a hand, fer too long. If he don't show soon, I predict he fell in the river after you hatcheted him an' drowned. River was in flood that night, an' the bank was slick. If he did fall in, I say good riddance."

In July of that summer, the Interstate Lumber Company transferred Percival Potts to Richmond, Virginia, and an older man was sent upriver from Grantsburg to replace him.

The summer waned and drifted into fall. Soon the countryside was ablaze with the handiwork of Jack Frost. Then, on a bright day in October, Biff Daggett stepped off the train in Stumpville.

At first glance, the stalwart lumberjack was the same man as of yore. But after close scrutiny, it was noticeable that an undefinable something had changed in his demeanor.

One of the first things he did after he alighted from the train was to inquire if Percival Potts was still around. When informed of the man's transfer, he smiled crookedly, fingering a long, ragged scar that ran from just below his right eye to clear to the edge of his craggy jaw.

"It's just as well," he muttered darkly, casting a baleful eye over the lounging bystanders. "That transfer saved Potts's neck. If he'd still been here, I was gonna kill him. As it is, I won't foller him up. But if he ever shows here again, and I'm around, look out."

Vouchsafing no information as to where he had been for half a year, he turned away. Picking up his bag, he stalked off down the street, his heavy hobnailed boots ringing hollowly on the wooden sidewalk.

Biff's former cronies wisely refrained from ever ribbing him again about his thwarted love for the beautiful Marcella Rand. They never brought up its disastrous outcome to him either. He had paid a terrible price in the game of love, they reasoned. Therefore, they felt they should not add to his burden of regret.

He would carry the disfiguring scar to his grave. And that, in itself, was adequate compensation for all the injustices they had suffered at his hands in the past.

A Red Letter Day

One clear, frosty morning in late September, more than twenty years ago, I told my father I was going squirrel hunting before leaving for the lower forty.

"But, son," he said, "you shouldn't waste time this morning on that sort of thing. The weather's perfect for us to finish digging our potatoes in the lower place."

"Look, Dad," I said with a laugh, "I won't be gone long. Cheer up. We'll get the potatoes dug and in the cellar before the day is over. Just bring me your old Bay State 16-gauge shotgun and a handful of shells. I'll be back by the time Mother has breakfast ready."

"All right," he agreed dubiously. "Go if you must. But I ain't going to hold my breath till you get back."

Knowing my fondness for squirrel hunting, my father didn't expect to see me, once I got into the woods, until hunger drove me home.

He went into the back bedroom and came out with the single-barreled shotgun I'd requested. He handed it to me and pulled three shells out of his pocket. He gave them to me with a wry look on his face.

"That's all the shells I've got," he said apologetically. "You can't have much of a hunt with only three loads for the gun, but it's the best I can do."

"Suppose I see more squirrels than I've got shells to take care of them with. What then?"

"Knock 'em outta the tree with rocks."

"Okay," I said with a laugh. "I'll take your advice. See you in less than an hour."

"I wouldn't bet on that," my father said with a grin, waving me away.

I quickly slipped on a denim jacket and hurried out of the house, heading toward the cow pasture. My destination was a fifty-acre wood lot that cornered the edge of a bluff that was a thousand feet or so up the creek from where we lived.

As I picked my way through the frost-covered grass, I could hear the squirrels barking and chattering in the woods up ahead. I could also hear another hunter blasting away about a mile or so down Old Camp Run. I

112

gave the old Bay State shotgun I carried a loving pat and hurriedly walked on. When I spotted the edge of the woods, I slowed my pace to creep cautiously forward.

Squirrels were sharp-eyed and sharp-eared little creatures. I had learned from past experience that the less noise I made while hunting them, the better my chances of success.

As soon as I entered the woods, I stopped. I peered all around me and listened until my ears ached. Not a sound broke the morning calm. The woods had suddenly become as silent as a tomb.

Knowing the habits of my furry friends quite well, I sat down on a nearby stump to wait. The squirrels were there. Of that, I was positive. I intended to wait quietly until their confidence was restored and they resumed their early morning activities up and down the trees.

I didn't have to wait long. Within five minutes, the woods around me seemed to come alive with frisking, barking, and nut-cutting squirrels.

About fifty feet from where I sat stood a huge beech tree. It had a top shaped like a gigantic umbrella. Suddenly, the tip of one of the branches facing me started shaking violently.

I stood silently, then crept forward. I was very careful as I did this. I knew that the slightest noise would send the squirrels into hiding again.

Soon I was able to see what it was that was shaking the branch so much. It was a nice fat squirrel, and he was busily cutting beechnuts.

As I stood and watched, I saw another branch that was also shaking quite a bit. It was on the far side of this huge old beech.

"Aah," I whispered. "So there's two of them up there having their breakfast. Well, I'm going to try for one of them, but which shall it be?"

Silently debating with myself as to which one to try for, I crept closer to the tree so as to get as good a shot as possible. Then I noticed an unusual thing about the two squirrels I was watching. By backing up a step or two, they became directly in line with each other.

Raising the old Bay State to my lips, I kissed the long black barrel. Then I slowly swung it up against my shoulder into firing position. Here before me was an opportunity that comes rarely, if ever, to a squirrel hunter. To kill two with one shot would entitle me to membership in the local two-for-one club. A distinction that I could tell of with pride for the rest of my life.

"Do your stuff, old girl," I whispered excitedly as I sighted along the top of the gun. *It's two for one for me this time, or I'm a knucklehead for sure.*

At the blast from the old Bay State, the woods sounded as if they were falling in around me. But I stood perfectly still and held my breath in hopeful expectation as I watched the two squirrels I had shot at. For a moment, nothing happened. Then slowly, reluctantly, the squirrel on the far side of the tree relaxed his hold on the branch and came tumbling down, to bounce on the leaves. I continued to wait and watch. Finally, the other one came crashing down.

"I did it, I did it," I yelled triumphantly as I danced a jig for joy.

I ejected the empty shell from the gun and replaced it with a good one. Then a squirrel began barking. I swung around and quickly spotted him about fifty feet away, sitting atop a big round sandstone boulder. His long, bushy tail flipped and jerked every time he barked.

Swinging the trusty old gun to my shoulder once more, I sighted down its barrel. At its full-throated roar, the squirrel tumbled off the rock and lay kicking in the leaves.

Picking up the dead game, I hurried out of the woods and down across the pasture to the house. My father met me on the back porch. Handing him the gun, and one shell, I pulled the squirrels out of my pockets. Smiling broadly, I laid them on the porch at his feet.

"What happened up there?" he asked as he looked at the gun, and the shell, and then, unbelievingly, at the three squirrels. "I only gave you three loads for the Bay State to start with. Now you give me back one shell, and you still got three of the bushy-tails to boot. I don't get it. Did you hit one over the head with the gun barrel?"

"Nope," I replied, keenly enjoying his bewilderment.

"How did you get him, then? Run him to death?"

"It was easy," I said with a laugh. "I took your suggestion seriously and knocked one out of the trees with a rock."

I gave my father a playful poke in the ribs before walking over to the yard pump to wash my hands. Then I walked into the kitchen to the hot breakfast I knew my mother would have waiting for me. I'd tell him the truth of my hunting experience later that day. But just for the moment, I decided to let him ponder over the mystery of how I had managed to kill three squirrels with only two shells.

The Ghost of Dead Man's Hollow

During my boyhood, down on the farm, it was a special treat for me and my sisters when our father was in a storytelling mood. Usually when such a fancy possessed him, it was on a snowy winter's night. And to our youthful imaginations, it seemed as though the howling wind from outside and the flickering firelight from the open hearth combined to weave a sense of magic into every thrilling word of the hair-raising stories he would tell.

On such occasions, he never failed to have this old, foul-smelling pipe stoked up and going full blast. Then, with his feet propped up on a homemade stool, he would lean back in his favorite chair, a huge splint-bottomed rocker, close his eyes, and, with the fragrant tobacco smoke swirling around his head, proceed to spin tales of bygone days that never failed to leave us children staring bug-eyed at one another.

Huddling close around our parents' feet, we would peer apprehensively into the shadows beyond the circle of light cast by the log fire. Even now, as I recall these frightening moments of long ago, I honestly believe we expected some ghoulish monster to come stalking out of the shadows to confront us.

One stormy night, after our father had finished telling a particularly spine-chilling story, he removed his pipe from his mouth, blew out a great cloud of smoke, and then asked us if we would like to hear the story of his first experience with a ghost.

"Oh yes, Dad," we said excitedly. "Please tell us. Oh please, *please.*"

"Promise you won't interrupt me," he demanded, winking at our mother to offset his grim manner.

"Cross our hearts and hope to die," we solemnly vowed.

"All right, then." He chuckled. "See that you kids keep your promise. If you don't, I'll stop right in the middle of the story and won't finish it."

He got up to place a fresh log on the smoldering fire and then resumed his position in the splint-bottomed rocker. Meeting each of our eyes to see that he had our undivided attention, he began his story.

"Well now, kids," he said, "this all happened years and years ago when I was a little shaver, no more than so big. At the time, Pap and Mother, and my brother, Frank, and my sister, Cora, and I lived up at the head of a deep, rocky hollow that emptied into the east fork of Duck Creek, just below Carlisle. This place was called Dead Man's Hollow.

"Old people in the community claimed it got its name from a white trapper who'd been murdered down at its mouth by the Indians years and years before.

"Anyway, about half a mile down the hollow from where we lived stood an old, abandoned log house. It was one of them big one-room affairs, like the settlers built when they homesteaded the land.

"Its windows were all knocked out. Even the window casings were gone. All that remained were the open places where the windows had been. Its one door was still there, but it was sagging at the hinges. The roof was slowly caving in, and the huge sandstone chimney that stood at the back of the house was crumbling. Saplings as thick as my body grew in the yard and garden spot.

"To me, this old decaying place was plenty spooky, even in broad daylight. At night, even the thought of it would turn my blood to ice.

"As I recall it now, I remember that nearly everybody in the neighborhood solemnly swore that the place was haunted. Someone or other had heard queer noises when they was passing there one night. And

121

they insisted that strange-looking lights had been seen around the old place by more than one person after dark.

"Well, Pap, Frank, and I, we hunted possums up and down Dead Man's Hollow every fall. But knowing how us boys felt about the old house, Pap never insisted we go by it while out night hunting with the dogs. And we never did.

"The only opening to the main road from where we lived was a rutty, rocky wagon road. And it ran right smack past that old devil of a house.

"During the school term, us kids passed that house twice a day going to and from the grade school on the fork. Sometimes, when we was late getting home from school, and the shadows of an early winter's night was already gathering there in the hollow, we'd have to go sloshing through the mud or snow past that old house. I must confess that most of the time I stared back over my shoulder at that old house till we went around a bend in the hollow and I couldn't see the haunted place anymore. Boy, I sure was brave in them days. Ha-ha."

We laughed with him.

"And then it happened," our father suddenly exclaimed. He laid aside his pipe and rose from his chair to stir up the fire.

"Go on, Dad," we pleaded. "Don't stop now."

"Hold your horses," he said, grinning. "First, I was thinking that maybe you kids ought to lug in a few more chunks of wood before they get all covered with snow. How about it? Do I hear any volunteers?"

At our father's words, our faces paled. We huddled even closer together and stared at him, aghast. When he saw the horrified looks on our faces, he gave a great bellow of laughter.

"Ha. *Ha*," he roared, slapping his leg in enjoyment. "Appears I've feathered myself a flock of chickens. But don't let it worry you none. I was a kid once myself. Forget about the wood. We've plenty for the night. I was just checking to see how the sand was holding out in your craws. From what I've seen, I'd say it's running a mite low. Wouldn't you?"

"Dad," Mother reproved him gently. "Remember, they're only children."

"I was only funning, a bit," he said, laughing. Then he patted her on the shoulder.

"Please tell us what happened to you at the old house in the hollow," we begged. Our father had interrupted his story at an exciting point and the suspense was making us squirm.

He just continued to laugh. Finally, he took a calming breath and said, "So you want to hear the rest of it, eh?"

"Yes, yes," we said eagerly.

"All right. I'll tell it. But hold onto your hair."

My father picked up his pipe, knocked the ashes out of it, and then reloaded it. Bending over, he grabbed a small glowing coal from the fireplace and placed it on the pressed-down tobacco in the pipe. Then he stuck the stem of his pipe between his lips and began to suck on it. In moments, great clouds of smoke escaped his mouth and swirled around his head. The old pipe was smoking like a locomotive.

"Now, as I was saying," he said as he reseated himself in the splint-bottomed rocker. "One Saturday afternoon in early December, when I was about ten, my mother sent me to the store down in Carlisle. I had to go alone, because Frank and Cora had the sore throat. Pap had gone rabbit hunting earlier in the day, and he wouldn't be back till darkness drove him home.

"I don't recall what prevented me from getting back home sooner than I did. Anyway, it was getting dark by the time I started up Dead Man's Hollow.

"When I realized how late it was, I broke into a trot, hoping to cover the mile or so to where we lived as quickly as I could. Most of the way was slightly upgrade. By the time I'd reached the little flat where the old house was, I was plenty winded.

"I paused a moment to catch my breath, then began pussyfooting past the house. My fear was nearly choking me.

"It was clear and cold that night; and a big round moon had just topped the ridge on the opposite side of the hollow. It shrouded the old place with an unreal sort of light that made it look awful to my ten-year-old eyes.

"So help me, that old house looked for all the world like some horrible monster of the past squatting there at the base of the hill in the shadow. Its two broken windows resembled big black vacant eyes, and the way they stared at me." He shivered here. "I shook as one afflicted with the ague."

My sisters and I huddled closer.

"When I was almost past that devil of a house, I heard it. Bump. Bump. Bump. *From inside the place.*

"The instant that sound fell on my ears, I froze. My hair even stood straight up on my head. Then I took off up the hollow like the wind. But I didn't run far.

"I wonder, even now, what made me stop and look back.

"The old tumbled-down house still sat there, bathed in the pale moonlight. As I stood and listened, I could still hear that bumping sound coming from inside it. Then something Pap had oftentimes told me popped into my mind.

"'Son,' Pap said, 'never run away from any queer sights and sounds you may see and hear after dark. If you can, always force yourself to investigate them. And I guarantee that what you thought was a ghost wasn't a ghost after all. It was only something you'd mistook for one in the dark.'

"Right then and there I made a decision—even though my teeth chattered with an awful fear as I made it. I knew that if I ran on home and told Pap about what I'd heard, then confessed I'd got cold fear and scooted instead of investigating, he'd look on me like I was a coward. And I don't think there's a boy living who wants his pap to think he's that.

"So, gritting my teeth, and shaking like a leaf, I started back to the old house to investigate the noise I'd heard.

"I mustered up courage I didn't know I had and shuffled along, my feet and legs so heavy that they felt as if they were made of solid iron. But I forced them to move in the right direction. I don't know how I did it, but I did.

"All too soon, I stood in the shadow of the old house. I looked up at the hollow-eyed windows. When I did this, I fought another battle with myself. I started sobbing with fear, and it seemed forever before I could force myself to climb up into one of the window openings. I couldn't get in through the door because it was fastened shut from the inside by something.

"Bump. Bump. Bump. That horrible sound came from right in front of me. Right then, my heart was making an even worse racket behind my ribs."

126

Our eyes widened in anticipation of his next words.

"It was pitch-black inside the old house. I struck a match and held it out in front of me, sobbing all the while. I said a prayer under my breath and tried to look inside. I was shaking so badly that the match almost went out. But it didn't. It flared up bright and clear. Then what do you think I saw?"

"What was it, Dad?" I whispered, horror stricken. My sisters were wide-eyed and silent. "Was it a ghost, or a goblin of some kind?"

"No," he replied.

We waited with bated breath. "Then it was the devil himself," I blurted in mortal terror, huddling closer to my sisters.

"Wrong again. It was neither ghost, nor goblin, nor devil."

"Tell us what it was. Oh, please," we entreated, clutching him with impatient hands in our anxiety.

"It was only a sheep."

"A sheep?" We couldn't believe our ears.

"That's right," our father laughingly assured us. "You see, a neighbor of ours, Big Henry Smith, pastured sheep down in the hollow below this old house. Evidently this one had gotten separated from the others, and it had gone into this old house thinking it was some kind of a shelter. It had gotten caught in some old, split-out tobacco sticks in one of the corners

127

and was kicking around trying to get loose. That was the bumping sound I'd kept hearing."

"What did you do then, Dad? Run on home?"

"Not just then," he replied. "First I climbed down from the window opening. Once inside the old house, I felt my way along the wall until I came to the sheep. After I got it loose from the tobacco sticks, I boosted it up and out of one of the windows. Then I climbed out and went on home.

"By the time I got home, my parents had begun to worry about me. But after I told them about what had happened down at the old house, I could see they was glad. Later that evening, Pap put his hands on my shoulders and said he was very proud of me. And it made me feel real good all over.

"I had met the challenge of fear, and I had come through it with flying colors. And to a small boy, out alone at night, a feat like that ain't to be sneezed at.

"During the rest of my boyhood days, and after I'd grown to manhood, I traveled those old hills and hollows on some of the darkest nights that ever existed. Not once did I ever see, or hear, anything that could truly be called a ghost. Pap always told me there wasn't such a thing, and my own experiences proved how right he was.

"And that," our father concluded with a chuckle, "is the story of the ghost that wasn't a ghost after all, but only a lost sheep."

Deflated Egotism

George Thompson swore disgustedly as he lay on his back in his friend Bill Riggs's backyard. With a shaking hand, he gingerly felt his swelling jaw.

"What the hell, Bill?" he complained, shaking his head to clear the fuzziness from his brain. "Did you have to whack me as hard as a mule could kick? You know I ain't no match for you with the gloves."

"I'm sorry, George," Bill said. Then he laughed, proving he wasn't. "Guess I just wasn't thinking when I clobbered you. I keep forgetting that you can't take the kind of punishment I'm capable of handing out when I start swinging. Here, let me help you up. From now on, I'll take it easy. No more dynamite. I promise."

"Your promises be hanged," George grumbled, getting unsteadily to his feet. Once he had found his balance, he began stripping off his boxing gloves. "I quit."

"Aw. Come on, pal," Bill implored. "I'll null 'em from now on. You won't get hurt. Honest, you won't. Man, can't you take even a little punishment?"

"Course I can. But I never felt more like a punching bag than I do right now. Besides, I got a date tonight. How would it look if I took Ruth out with me sporting a shiner?"

Bill laughed in merriment as he danced around, shadowboxing an imaginary foe. "Loosen up and live a little. Don't be an old woman all your life."

"Find someone else to pummel. I got to be going. It's after six, and Ruth's expecting me at seven thirty. In the meantime, I've got to try and get my jaw back in place. See you later."

"Bye, champ," Bill said as his friend left. Bill and George were friends of long standing. They were born and raised on adjoining farms along the Ohio River Valley, and they had attended the same schools. After trying their hands at various jobs, they finally decided to give shop work a whirl. It paid better than most outside jobs, but, like all outside employment, the weather played a major role in the number of days one could work. Shop work, however, was steadier than some of the other jobs they'd had. And for the last three years, the young friends had had steady employment at a roller mill in Cambridge, Ohio.

George was never the sportsman type; but Bill was an avid fan of all forms of athletics, especially boxing. Soon all his friends and fellow workers came to the realization that Bill was just too nimble with the gloves to spar with. His relentless hammering was no longer amusing, and they did not particularly care for black eyes, loose teeth, and swollen jaws.

As time went by, Bill became more and more convinced of his powers with the gloves. He also developed an unpleasant cockiness that was distasteful to all who knew him.

George Thompson, needless to say, remained true to their longstanding friendship. As Bill's head began to swell with a false sense of his ability, George's estimation of his friend's worth was still as staunch as ever.

Look, fellows, Bill's a good sort," he would stoutly maintain whenever the men at the shop complained about Bill and his obnoxious behavior. "It's just that he's put too much stock in that boxing stuff he's hipped with. Once he's lost interest for it, everything'll be the same as before. Why not give him a chance? Just wait and see."

"Quit sticking up for that swelled head," one man would grumble while the rest nodded in agreement. They all remembered the many times

Bill had called them chicken when they refused to box with him. "He needs his block knocked off. And his own gloves to boot. Maybe that'd teach him some sense."

"You're absolutely right. And I'm hoping and praying for the same thing. Maybe he'll buck up against the wrong man one day. We can hope."

Another offensive trait Bill soon began to exercise was an antagonistic attitude toward new employees. Whenever a new man was hired, Bill would immediately give him the once-over. If the new employee was young enough, and strong enough, to be a possible contender for the cock-of-the-walk position Bill fancied he occupied, he would issue an immediate challenge to do battle.

To accept such a challenge was to lay one's self open to a merciless hammering from a man with sledgehammer fists. Consequently, it was not unusual for a new man to walk away from his new job rather than submit to such treatment.

One day in midsummer, a new face appeared in the shipping room. Timothy Sullivan was a young Irishman of likeable nature. Short and broad, he possessed an unusual amount of muscle in his arms and shoulders. Soon some of the old-timers in the plant began to talk among themselves. They said that "Irish," as they had dubbed young Sullivan, could give Bill a run for his money if only he was a mite taller.

"Too bad Irish is so short," one said and they all agreed regretfully. "What wouldn't we give to see a nice lad like him clean Bill's plow."

In time, this plant gossip reached Bill's ears and he took another look at young Sullivan. Then he threw back his head and roared with laughter.

"I don't fight boys," he told the old-timers. "Irish is only a wet-eared kid. If I challenged him to a boxing match, I'd look like a louse." Then to young Sullivan he said, "Relax man. There ain't gonna be any battle."

During the weeks that followed this encounter, Bill and Tim became friends. Soon Bill was inviting the young Irishman to put gloves on and join him for just a bit of practice. But the boyish Tim always laughingly declined.

"It ain't as though I'm going to hurt you, Irish," Bill would patiently point out. "So I don't see why you're so leery. Look, have them ginks at the shop been feeding you a line of bull about me?"

"Could be, Bill, could be. Mainly, though, it's because I'm not overly fond of having my eyes blackened and my teeth knocked loose. Let's face it. You're just too much of a man for a runt like me."

"Guess you're one of them chicken-livered characters too," Bill would say with a sneer, hoping the slighting remark would needle Tim into putting the boxing gloves on. But Tim Sullivan seemed immune to the many insults Bill cast at him.

"Now I wouldn't say I'm a chicken. No sirree, I sure wouldn't."

"Hogwash, Irish. What else can I think? You ain't no weakling."

"That's right," Tim readily agreed. "I'm in pretty good shape, and I'd like to stay that way. If I let you pummel me like you do the others, I won't be. Pick yourself another sucker. I'm wise to your game. Ha-ha."

On certain days, the shipping-room employees worked an hour later than the rest of the shop. And oftentimes, Bill would be out in his backyard shadowboxing when Tim went by on his way home from work.

The boardinghouse where he lodged was on the next street over from Bill's place, and, on such occasions, Bill never failed to extend an invitation to stop and box a round or two with him. But Tim would always laugh cheerfully, shake his head no, and continue on his way.

One hot, humid Friday evening in late August, Tim was later than usual going past on his way home from work. When he did appear on the street, Bill and George were in the backyard boxing. As soon as Bill sighted his Irish friend, he ceased pummeling George and, smiling broadly, extended his usual invitation for Tim to try a round or two with him.

"Pull up there, Tim boy," he shouted. "You're in luck. You're just in time to put on some mitts for a whirl with your uncle Bill. And this time, I'm not taking any of your flimsy excuses."

"You're looking great, Bill," Tim said with a grin, his blue eyes

136

twinkling. "Top form, as usual. How's George standing up under your haymakers?"

"No damn good," George replied sourly. "This guy is about as pleasant to spar with as an octopus. While I'm figuring out how to evade his straight rights, he nails me with that left hook he's so good at."

"Well, maybe you'll outwit him yet," Tim said cheerfully. "When you do, hand him a couple of belly punches to even the score up a little."

"That'll be the day," Bill said with a grin, enjoying the situation immensely. "See here now, Irish. Put 'em on. I mean to have a round with you this evening—even if I have to knock you down and put the gloves on myself."

"Sorry, friend, but I'm begging off again. Surely a big strong fellow like you wouldn't pick on a little guy like me. How would it look?"

"To hell with how it looks," Bill snapped, his temper flaring. "All I'm asking is for us to spar a bit. And as usual, you chicken out on me. You make me sick, Irish. Honest you do. Get out of my sight. Get on over to Ma Dodds's boardinghouse. Your diaper needs changing."

"Easy, Bill, easy," Tim cautioned, a hint of steel in his usually pleasant voice. "Keep handing out the insults and I'll have to pin your ears back yet. I tossed off a couple of quick slugs of red-eye down at the bar after I knocked off work. So speak softly when you're talking to me. I'm not overly fond of your loud-mouthed way of abusing your friends. Understand, *pal?*"

"Ha. *Ha*," Bill cried. "So the hooch has bolstered up your courage, eh? Got some sand in your craw now. Is that it? Well, I just dare you to put the gloves on. If you do, I'll hammer that noggin of yours like a ripe melon. What do you say to that, Irish?"

"Nuts to you," Tim answered, setting down his lunch pail and holding out his hands to George. "Lace 'em on, George. Make sure they're on good and tight. When I swing at this big lug, I don't want one to fly off. Reckon it's about time I tangled with him."

"Forget it, Irish," George said. "Bill suckered you into this. Can't you see that? Go on home. He'll beat you into a jelly. It'd be suicide for you to take him on. You're out of your mind."

But all of George's pleading fell on deaf ears. Timothy Sullivan insisted that he lace the boxing gloves on him. He also insisted that George lace Bill's on too.

When the gloves were on tight, the short Irishman held out a gloved hand and grinned up at his towering opponent.

"All right now, Bill," he said, chuckling. "Reckon this is what you've been waiting for. There's only one thing though."

"What's that, Irish?" Bill asked, smiling broadly. "Want to tell me where to ship your remains in case this bout proves fatal?"

"Have your fun while you can, but that ain't what I had in mind. It's only this. Strike at me just as hard as you can. That's how I'm going to do it with you. Fair enough?"

"Sure is, only I better pull 'em a little. I wouldn't want to hurt a half-pint like you. I'd never live the disgrace of it down. Don't worry, Irish. I won't bung you up too badly."

"I'll take that chance," Tim said with simple dignity. "**WHEN YOU FEEL FROGGIE, JUMP**!!! I'm ready and waiting."

With a whoop of joy, Bill swooped down on his boyish opponent, his huge fists churning like a pile driver. It looked as though he was going to pulverize the opposition with one devastating blow, but Tim stepped aside at the last second. As Bill went charging past, Tim shot out his right glove. It landed with a solid thud against the bigger man's jaw.

Bill's head snapped back, and he was knocked sprawling.

"My foot slipped, Irish," he mumbled, picking himself up off the grass. "But I'll get you this time."

"Reckon you will at that," Tim agreed pleasantly as he stood calmly by while Bill regained his feet. Without warning, Bill charged.

Again, it looked as though the smaller man was doomed. But as before, he was able to dodge Bill's wild rush at the last instant and drive a sharp blow into the man's midriff.

As Bill bent over in agony, Tim hit him with another precision-like left. The blow connected with Bill's jaw and down he went, again. This time he fell right at George's feet. As he lurched up, a wide grin split George's homely features.

"What's wrong, pal?" he said. "From where I'm standing, I'd say you've either met your match or you're having a bad afternoon. Now which is it? You gonna stand up and fight, or not?"

"I'll murder him," Bill growled, gathering himself for another wild charge.

As he bore down on his boyish opponent, Tim rushed to meet him. Again, the Irishman ducked his head at the last moment, and Bill's brawny right arm swept harmlessly over his shoulder, cleaving nothing but thin air.

Tim brought a whistling uppercut through Bill's flailing arms. It landed on the point of the bigger man's jaw with a sharp crack. Needless to say, Bill hit the grass again. This time, he was out as cold as poleaxed beef.

"Great balls of fire," George whispered as he stared in bug-eyed disbelief at his fallen friend. "What did you knock him with that time, Irish? A sledgehammer?"

140

"Nope. Only my right glove," Tim said, laughing. "Get a bucket of water, George. I ain't through with this big bully yet."

Smiling broadly, George quickly brought the requested water. At Tim's instruction, he unceremoniously dumped it on Bill's upturned face.

"Whatsa matter, whatsa matter?" Bill spluttered, sitting up and wiping the cold water from his face as best he could with the boxing gloves. "What happened?"

"Get up, you big windbag," Tim ordered. "You gone chicken on me?"

"Hell no," Bill roared, staggering to his feet. "I can't seem to stay on my feet. But I ain't through with you, Irish. Not by a long shot. I slipped that time, and you was lucky. I'll nail you before this is over."

"Stop flapping that loud mouth of yours and show me. So far all you've been doing is rolling down the lawn. Stand up and fight."

Bill bore down on his boyish opponent again and again, only to be met with bone-jarring rights and lefts that upended him every time.

"Try this one on your long nose," Tim yelled. "How does this one suit your big mouth? Here's a good one for that fat gut of yours."

Thus it went. Without exception, Tim Sullivan hit his towering opponent whenever, and wherever, he chose. At last, Bill staggered back and covered his bruised face and bleeding nose with his gloves. He was shaking like a leaf in a high wind, and his breath came in ragged gasps.

"Don't hit me again, Irish," he pleaded. "If you do, I believe it'll kill me."

"Had enough?"

"Yes, yes."

"Still think you're cock of the walk around here?"

"No I don't."

"Good." Tim laughed. "Reckon you had the impression you was quite a man. Now didn't you?"

"Yes I did. Right now, though, I'm feeling like two cents. I can't figure out how you did what you did to me."

"It's simple enough. Look, pal, ever since I got hired on at the mill, I've been hearing about how handy you think you are with the gloves. Do you still think that?"

"Not anymore," Bill grunted, wiping his bloody nose with one of the gloves.

"Then take a tip from me. You ain't got it when it comes to pushing leather. Give it up before you really get hurt."

"Why do you say that, Irish?"

"Experience" was his straightforward reply as he held out his hands for George to unlace the gloves. Bill had the feeling that there was something about Timothy Sullivan that the general public did not know.

His thoughts must have shown on his face, because Tim said, "All right, I'll tell you. But it's a part of my life that I'd like to forget. It's like this. I too once had the impression that I was a damn good little man, and quite a whiz with the gloves. But one night in Cleveland, about three years ago, I found out different. That night, I boxed for bantamweight championship of the world. When I woke up, I'd swallowed four of my teeth. Right then and there I changed my mind about the gloves. Good day, fellows. See you at the shop next week."

Picking up his lunch pail, the unassuming little Irishman strode out of the yard and continued on his way to the boardinghouse.

"Well I'll be," Bill muttered as he watched him stride away. "Look, George, I'm asking a favor of you. Keep what happened here under your hat. Okay? If you blab it around, I'll be the laughingstock of the shop, and the guys will razz me to hell and gone. Man, but can that runt of a Tim hit hard. It felt like he had rocks in them gloves."

"How about this boxing stuff now, Bill?" George asked. "Still going to try and push the fellows around after what happened here just now?"

"No, I'm not."

"Then perhaps you see things differently?" George pressed. What he had long waited for had finally come to pass. And he fervently hoped his friend had learned a well-deserved lesson.

"Yes, George. I see clearly now for the first time in a long while. Tim was right. I ain't got no business fooling around with this sort of thing. He convinced me of that in about five minutes. Little as Irish is, he could've really hurt me if he'd wanted to. As it is, he damned near knocked me to pieces. And he was only keeping away from me most of the time. What if he'd wanted to clobber me good?"

"That's right," George agreed, secretly delighted at the drubbing his friend had received. "You'd be playing it smart to forget this boxing nonsense. Actually, you're lucky. Lots of fellows lose an eye or wind up punch-drunk for the rest of their lives before it gets through to them that they ain't got what it takes to be a champion."

Not long afterward, Bill got rid of his boxing gloves, much to the amazement of his fellow workers. When they questioned him about his decision, he shook his head and smiled, vouchsafing no information.

He had learned a hard, but true, lesson. No one is so strong because there is always someone who is stronger. And no one is so accomplished at any given thing because there is always someone who is better at it.

They Call Him Bull

It was on a day in mid-April, more than a score of years ago, that I had my introduction to Bull. Earlier that spring, my family and I had moved to a little village in southern Ohio to tend the local telephone switchboard.

Lebanon boasted but one main street. And at times, when I walked it to the general store, I would see a black-and-white bulldog in the backyard of one of the well-kept homes that lined the street.

Our next door neighbors quickly warned me that this dog was a "bad one," and they hinted strongly that I'd be playing it smart to steer clear of him at all times.

So far luck had been with me. In the six weeks we had been living in Lebanon, I had not met this dog face-to-face.

On this particular day, I was on my way to the store to purchase some fishing supplies when I saw him lying on the flagstone sidewalk in front of the big white house where I had seen him in the backyard.

With a feeling of apprehension gripping me, I walked on, hoping fervently as I did so that when I came close he would get up and move out of my way. I soon realized, however, that that was not going to be the case.

Closer, and closer, I trudged. And still the dog lay there unperturbed, as though no one was within a mile of him. When less than a dozen feet separated us, he turned his head and looked at me. I saw hate and distrust in his big brown eyes, and I quickly decided to make overtures of friendship.

"Hello, doggie," I said in a quavering voice as I stepped off the sidewalk to walk around him. As I spoke, I held out my right hand and snapped my fingers.

His reaction to my gesture of friendliness was exactly as the neighbors had said it would be. Growling viciously, he sprang to his feet and glared at me with baleful eyes, his teeth bared in a grimace of hate.

Taken aback by the dog's sudden display of hostility, I retreated a few steps and paused in indecision. Should I continue to the store on that side of the street, I asked myself, or should I cross over and go down on the other side?

As I mentally debated my dilemma, I heard a man calling to me from behind. "Hey there, boy. Is my dog giving you a bad time?"

Turning around, I looked into the keen blue eyes of a tall man of advanced years. With a word and wave of his hand, this stranger immediately quieted the dog.

"Not yet," I answered shakily. "But he sure scared the daylights outta me just now."

"Reckon he's been having that same effect on folks hereabouts for quite a spell," drawled the oldster.

"What's his name?" I asked.

"We call him Bull."

"Just Bull?" I asked in amazement.

"That's right," the old man replied.

With a grin, I acknowledged that the dog was aptly named. Even with such a short acquaintance as I had had with him, I could see that he possessed the ferocious nature of a cross bull.

"Yeah," the old man said apologetically, "Bull's definitely on the unfriendly side these days. By the way, boy, what's your name?"

"Bud," I said.

"Bud, huh," he said musingly. "Well, Bud, I'm Mart Doan. Now tell me how old you are."

"Ten."

"Guess you're the right age to be interested in dogs. Only I wouldn't advise it in Bull's case."

"Why not?"

"Too dangerous, boy. That's why not. He's not to be trusted around kids anymore."

"What's wrong with him?" I persisted. "Why is he so cross and unfriendly all the time?"

"You can lay the blame on the older boys in this burg," Mart Doan explained. "Ever since he was a pup, they've clubbed him, thrown rocks at him, and chased him. So much so, that it's been years now since he's trusted a living soul. Lately he don't even cotton to me like he should. If that keeps up, I'm afraid I'll have to get rid of him."

"Maybe I can make friends with Bull," I suggested hopefully. The thought of winning the friendship of this deeply distrusting dog fired my youthful imagination, and I ached to try.

"Don't take chances with him, boy," Mr. Doan cautioned. "You'll only be running unnecessary risks if you do, and you might get dog bit to boot."

150

"Mind if I try?" I asked eagerly.

"Nope," the old man replied. "Just remember what I told you."

With the confidence of the very young, I completely ignored the old man's warning and centered my attention on the dog. At the moment, he was watching a big black bug that was laboriously making its way along the side of one of the flagstones in the sidewalk. From the moment his master had appeared, Bull had not paid the slightest attention to me.

"Come, Bull," I called coaxingly.

As before, my friendly overture went for naught. Bull abandoned his interest in the black bug and gave a low growl of rage. Jerking his head up, he snapped his powerful jaws shut with a sharp click, like that of a sprung steel trap.

"Get to the house, you black devil," Mr. Doan snapped as he aimed a kick at the dog. Bull expertly dodged the heavy shoe and stalked out of reach of his master. Then he began trotting up the walk to the big white house.

"That's what I mean, son," the old man said with a sigh of resignation. "In the future, keep clear of that mutt. You'll be courting trouble if you don't."

"He's awful bad and mean," I whispered to myself as I continued on to the store. "But maybe I can win him over. I ain't got a dog of my own now, and I'll bet he'd make a fine pet."

To win the trust of this dog who had become alienated against all humans presented a great challenge to me. And with typical boyhood zest, I accepted that challenge gladly.

During the months that followed, however, I was often reminded of what Mart Doan had told me. All my efforts to make friends with Bull fell flat. Not once did he fail to advertise his animosity toward me. And oftentimes, when I allowed my enthusiasm for friendship with him to get out of hand, I narrowly escaped being bitten.

Eventually, though, his belligerence subsided somewhat. But I soon discovered that he had only slightly relaxed his vigilance, and nothing more. Whenever I approached him, his big brown eyes would regard me with distrust. Then he would growl ominously at me and retreat with stiff-legged dignity to the sanctuary of his master's backyard.

I always interceded on Bull's behalf whenever I saw him being mistreated by the older boys of the village, but my pleas for clemency for

him fell on deaf ears. Every time they caught Bull away from home, they never failed to work their devilment on him with merciless glee. Roaring his hate for them, Bull would dash for home, leaving a trail of sticks, stones, and clods of dirt behind him.

At last, in desperation, I sought out my father and asked for his help and guidance in my campaign to win Bull's friendship. I had failed miserably on my own, I knew, and I grudgingly admitted that I needed the advice of a parent.

"Take it easy with him, Bud," my father advised.

"Jerusalem, Dad," I said in exasperation, "I'm moving like a snail with this crazy dog, and he's still as cross and unfriendly as he was the day of our first run-in."

"Okay, then," my father said with a laugh. "Try giving him the independent treatment for a while and see how he reacts."

"What good would that do?" I asked disgustedly.

"You never can tell. At least don't coax him anymore. If he wants to thaw out, he'll do it on his own or not at all."

"I'll try it, Dad," I said as new hope surged up in my young heart. Hope springs eternal in the hearts of all youngsters, and in those days, I was no exception.

Thereafter I employed my father's advice to the fullest. No more did I extend a hand and snap my fingers whenever I saw Bull. All I did was speak to him and immediately walk on.

After a few weeks, I began to notice a change. His animosity gradually gave way to curiosity. Whenever I would casually walk past him, he would cant his head at an amusing angle and gaze after me with a look on his homely face that I interpreted as perplexity.

153

When I saw this, I smiled triumphantly. He was weakening. Soon he would be licking my hands instead of acting like he wanted to snap them off. I discovered shortly after, though, that my victory over Bull's obstinacy was far from being won.

■■■

Summer receded into fall, and fall gradually gave way to winter's frigid hand, and still Bull treated me with the same aloofness that he had from the start. Not once during all those months did he give the slightest indication that he wanted to be friends with me. Then suddenly, and with no advance warning whatsoever, the unexpected happened.

On a cold Saturday afternoon in late January, I heard something timidly scratching at our kitchen door. I went to the door and looked outside. What I saw caused me to stare in disbelief.

There on our doorstep stood Bull. Concealing my surprise as best I could, I said, "Why hello, Bull. Come right in."

He gave no sign that he heard my greeting. He just looked me over with the solemnness of a judge about to pass sentence. For a long moment after, he simply stood there, his posture rigid. I repeated my invitation.

With a shake of his head, and a deciding kind of a snort, he trotted past me into the kitchen, then continued on into the living room.

In the living room, he scrutinized my parents and sisters with his solemn big brown eyes. Apparently satisfied with what he saw, he walked over to the fireplace and lay down on the hearth. Almost immediately, he got back up and trotted over to the kitchen door.

"Let him out," my father called from the living room. "But don't worry. He'll be back."

"That dog's got me running around in circles, Dad," I said. "Ever since we met, he's done nothing but give me the cold shoulder. He almost bit me several times too. And only because I tried to make friends with him. Now all of a sudden he comes to the house and wants in. Honestly, I don't understand him at all."

"Don't let Bull's behavior fool you," my father said. "Coming here today was his way of telling you that he wants to be friends just as much as you do."

"I don't believe he meant that at all," I muttered.

"It's true, son," my father assured me, "be patient with him. And above all things be kind. You'll not be sorry in the long run if you do."

Every day thereafter Bull came to my home and scratched on the door for admittance. Gradually he lengthened his visits until some days he would spend more than an hour by our fireside.

155

A fortnight later, I chanced to meet him on the street again. Putting on my cheeriest smile, I called his name and held out a hand.

"Here, Bull," I called hopefully. "Come to me, boy."

Once more the effect of the years of ill treatment he had received came to the fore. Eyeing me with distrust, he gave me one of those vicious growls I had come to know so well. And with raised bristles, he stalked away.

"Dog, I give up with you," I said deeply chagrined.

That evening as I recounted the experience to my father, he threw an arm around my shoulders in parental understanding and nodded his head sagely.

"I know exactly how you feel, Bud," he said simply. "But don't give up. Patience and kindness will turn the trick with Bull yet."

"Patience, patience," I grumbled. "That's all you ever say, Dad. I'm about ready to call it quits."

"Easy now," he cautioned. "You're nearer your goal than you think. I'm willing to wager that any day now you'll see a complete change in that dog's attitude toward you."

"I doubt it."

"Look at it this way," my father said. "Bull wouldn't keep coming to the house every day like he's been doing if he wasn't on the verge of giving over. Animals aren't built that way."

"But how will I know when he's changed his mind about me?"

"You'll know," my father said. "When he accepts you, it'll be all the way. There won't be any doubt in your heart then about his intentions."

My father's words of wisdom proved correct. Later that same week, I encountered Bull in the street again. The day was dark and gloomy, and it was snowing quite heavily. When I saw him, he was nosing around the roots of a large elm tree across the street from where I was walking.

Determined not to pass up an opportunity in my campaign to win his friendship, I gave a low whistle and called. This time I also held out a hand like I had so many times in the past. Then a miracle happened.

With a yipping bark, Bull came bounding across the snowy street. And without the slightest hesitation whatsoever, he sprang straight into my arms. I was speechless. All I could do was clasp his wriggling form to me, while he profusely licked my face and hands with his red tongue.

Then he wiggled out of my arms and began cavorting around me, kicking joyously at every jump. Gone completely was his former hostility. In that moment, Bull had become like a pup again. With tears in my eyes and a lump in my throat, I knelt to pet him as I had dreamed of doing for close to a year. His response to my every touch was as loving and trusting as a little child.

From that day forward, we were friends. The other boys in the little village couldn't believe their eyes when they saw how he had taken to me. Kindness was the answer, I could have told them. But instead, I held my peace. Their inhuman treatment had alienated him against all humanity. And knowing this, I felt that they did not rate an explanation.

Many years have rolled over my head since I last saw Bull. And I know that his bones were long ago laid to rest. But I shall never forget that lonely, distrustful dog, who, after he had closed his heart to all mankind, finally capitulated unconditionally to the healing balm of a small boy's kind words and gentle hands.

The Reward of Patience

The midsummer sun was setting when Clint Johnson walked the last few steps to the crest of the ridge and sat down on a rock to take a breather. As he mopped the sweat from his brow, he turned and gazed down into the valley he had just climbed out of.

Through the gathering shadows in the valley below, he could see the top of the drilling rig. The creaks and groans of it operating drifted up to him quietly on the balmy summer air.

Jack and Dave were going full steam ahead as he had instructed them, and his heart swelled with pride as he thought of the loyalty they had shown him through all the bitter disappointments he had sustained during the past five years.

Already they were at the top of the last pay sand they could reach with the equipment he had, and so far the well had been dry as a bone. With a heavier outfit they could go much deeper, Clint knew, but even as he thought this, he knew it was only wishful thinking. His old rig would never stand the strain.

After a few moments, he got up off the rock and stretched some of the stiffness out of his lanky frame. He ran his fingers through his sandy hair in thought, then he put on his battered felt hat and resumed his journey with a look of defeat in his blue eyes.

"What's the use of all this rat race anyway?" he muttered disgustedly as he made his way down the rocky path on the other side of the ridge. "Sometimes I feel like I've been playing with a stacked deck these past five years."

Dropping down into the valley ahead, he began walking up the public road that ran past his father's two-hundred-acre farm. Even with a feeling of hopelessness still riding him, he walked fast, and in half an hour he was knocking on his father's front door.

"Come in," Amos Johnson's booming voice sounded from the living room. At the sound of that authoritative voice, Clint again considered the futility of his visit to his father's house.

He took a deep breath and opened the screen door. "Hello, Dad," he said, stepping into the living room. "And Mom. How's everybody?"

"We're fine, Clint," his mother said, smiling.

"Evenin', son," Amos Johnson rumbled while his eagle eyes gave Clint a quick once-over.

"You look kind of peaked, boy," his mother observed with the ever-present concern of a mother for her only son. "Haven't you been feeling well lately?"

"I'm okay, Mom," Clint answered, casting a sidelong glance at his father as he spoke. "I do feel lousy, but my troubles ain't all physical by any means."

"Well, come on out to the kitchen, and I'll fix you a cup of coffee," his mother said. "Whatever your troubles are, I'm sure a good cup of hot coffee will brighten you up a bit."

"That'll be fine, Mom," Clint said, grinning at her.

"And another thing," she said, smiling at him happily, "Pa and me had apple pie for supper. It's your favorite, I know, and there's a big piece left that you can have with your coffee."

"I'll be right out," Clint promised. "But first I've something to ask of Dad."

His father had been silently eyeing him with the discerning eyes of a parent, and his face hardened noticeably at Clint's words. Amos Johnson knew from the greasy work clothes Clint was wearing that his son's visit was not a social one.

"Go fix the coffee, Mother," Amos Johnson said as he stood up from the splint-bottomed rocker he had been sitting in. He then proceeded to fill and light his pipe. "I'll see what's got Clint so down in the mouth."

As soon as Mrs. Johnson retired to the kitchen, the rugged old farmer turned to Clint. "All right, boy," he grunted, "out with it. What's on your mind? What have you come for this time?"

Knowing the uselessness of trying to hedge his words with his father, Clint simply stated the purpose of his visit. "I need some money, Dad."

"How much?"

"At least fifty dollars," Clint answered, staring at the granite-hard face before him.

"Uh-huh, I see," his father muttered. "Now tell me this. Just what do you plan on doing with the fifty dollars you're asking me to lend you?" "I need it for the well I'm drilling," Clint reluctantly told his father. "So," Amos Johnson growled, "you're planning on sinking it into that worthless hole in the ground. Am I right?"

"That's about the size of it, Dad," Clint shamefully acknowledged. "I plan on giving Jack and Dave some of it though. They're family men, same as me. But I'd planned on most of the money going as part payment for some good used tubing I heard of yesterday."

"Never," the old man said, shaking a finger under his son's nose. "For anything worthwhile I'd give you any reasonable amount of money you asked me for. But I'll be doggoned if I'll give you another red cent to sink into anymore of your dry holes. And that's final."

"But what about Jack and Dave?" Clint implored. "They've got families to worry about. I've got to pay them something tonight. It's Saturday, and they need groceries for the coming week."

"That's their hard luck," Amos Johnson told his son with a flinty smile. "I say that since they've chosen to cast their lot with you in your rainbow chasing then let them bear the consequences of their folly."

"But look, Dad," Clint said in desperation, "oil in paying quantities is being found every day."

"Sure it is" was Amos Johnson's immediate reply. "Look, son, it takes a barrel of money, and more luck than sense, to succeed in that game. And you know as well as I do that you don't have either of those. You're just not cut out to be an oil man."

"Look at it from my side of the fence," Clint pleaded. "Just because my luck's been bad in the past is no guarantee it'll continue to be rotten in the future."

"I'll grant you that," the older man said. "Only here's the rub. You're in no position to chase rainbows any longer. It's high time you forgot this wild scheme of becoming an oil man and settled down to something that's certain. Dreams are for kids. Not men with families to support."

"The oil business is all I know," Clint said.

"Correction," Amos Johnson snapped, "the drilling business is all you've known. You haven't seen any oil."

"But all that could change with this well I'm drilling now."

"Don't make me laugh," his father said. "How long have you been chasing this rainbow of yours?"

"Almost six years," Clint muttered.

"All right, then tell me something else while we're on the subject. How many wells, or should I say dry holes, have you dug for yourself in that time?"

"Twelve. The one I'm finishing up now will make thirteen," Clint said, the disappointment of those fruitless years heavy in his voice. "And

how much money have those dry holes paid you so far?" "Nothing, as

yet," Clint admitted, knowing even as he did so what his

father's next words would be.

"And you still insist on sinking more money into this pipe dream of yours?" the old man said in disbelief.

"That's right, I do. Dad, I know it's impossible for you to see this thing in the same light as I do. For years now I've been going ahead on faith, faith that there's something down there worth going after. That may sound silly to you, but that's the way I feel about my search for oil."

"Poppycock," Amos Johnson said, snorting in disgust. "Son, wake up. You're in debt up to your eyebrows. And you've nothing to show for your efforts but the experience, and that debt. What will it take to make you see the light?"

"You're right," Clint admitted. "But that don't change the way I feel one little bit."

"You owe everybody and his brother who loaned you a thin dime to help you in this wild goose venture. I'm telling you, son, that you're headed for financial ruin. You've even mortgaged your home to help finance this crazy scheme. Can't you realize that you've reached the end of your rope?"

Just then Mrs. Johnson called from the kitchen to say that the coffee was ready and waiting.

"I may sound like a fool," Clint said doggedly, "but before I call it quits, I want to see the rainbow colors on a drill bit that came out of a well I've drilled. That's the least I can ask for."

"Well, at the rate you've been going, you'll probably be in the poorhouse when that happens," his father said as they walked into the kitchen. "Mother, pour me another cup of coffee. I need it to wash a bad taste out of my mouth."

A few minutes later, Clint took leave of his parents. He carried his mother's well wishes with him, but his father's emphatic refusal to loan him more money still rang in his ears.

A silvery moon sailed high in the sky and cast soft shadows around him as he walked, mentally kicking himself as he visualized the naked disappointment on Jack's and Dave's faces when he would have to tell them that he had returned empty-handed.

Both of them had been intensely loyal to him throughout all the fruitless searches for oil in paying quantities, and it galled him unmercifully to have to part company with them. If this well proved to be another duster, Clint knew beyond the shadow of a doubt that the jig was up for him.

Only the week before, the banker in Marietta had curtly informed him that unless he came up with something tangible, and very soon, they were planning an immediate foreclosure. The directors, the banker had said, were through doing business with someone with nothing more substantial than promises to go on.

As he mulled this ominous ultimatum over in his mind, he slowly climbed the rocky path to the crest of the ridge above the drilling well. When he reached the crest of the ridge, he stood a moment to listen if the men were still drilling. The rhythmic creak and groan of the straining outfit floated up to him from the valley below. Intermingling with these sounds, he heard the ringing beat of a sledgehammer on a drill bit.

Clint Johnson smiled without humor when he heard the sounds of activity below. Jack was running out another screw, and Dave was sharpening a bit. Both were carrying on as though their wages had been paid in full to date, instead of being more than a month in arrears.

God, he silently prayed as he gazed at the starlit heavens, *please let this well be the payoff for all the disappointments that the other wells have brought. I ask not for myself alone, but for my men. I want their faith in me to be justified.*

He resumed walking down the rugged slope and quickly came to the valley floor. Stealing his face to hide the failure of his mission from their eagle eyes, he hurried to the rig and strode onto the drilling floor.

167

"Hey, boss," Jack hailed him from his position on the driller's stool. "Did you jar your old man loose for a bit of the long green?"

Dave waved a hand in greeting from by the forge and silently waited for a reply to Jack's question. What was the use of trying to put up a front with these two, Clint asked himself. After nearly six years of working with them, he knew that each had eyes sharp enough to penetrate boiler plate. So, with a shake of his head and a shrug of his shoulders, he blurted out the unfortunate truth. "The jig is up. Dad wouldn't loan me another dime. Looks like you'll have to go home empty-handed again."

"That's no great disaster, boss," Dave said calmly as he squared his heavy shoulders and rearranged the overalls on his squat figure. "We've still got plenty to eat at home yet. Got a garden full of vegetables to pick from too."

"Same here," Jack said. "We can string along for quite a while if we have to. My credit's still good down at the Fork's, and I'll see that Dave can get groceries on my slip there if he needs them."

"No," Clint snapped. "Can't you two get it through your thick heads what I'm trying to say?"

"Reckon not," Dave replied, grinning at him crookedly. "I can't see why you're so down at the mouth. Cheer up. This ain't the first time we've been on the ragged edge. Yet you look like you've been invited to your own funeral."

"My funeral couldn't be more depressing than our present situation," Clint muttered. He looked at Jack. "Tell me, Jack, how far have you drilled into the sand?"

"A little over fifteen feet."

"Any sign of anything yet?"

"Nothing" was the laconic reply. "So far she's been as dry as a bone."

"How much sand is left to drill through?"

"Possibly another eight or ten feet. Offhand, though, I'd say about another screw."

"That's just what I mean," Clint said as he stepped to the driller's side and shut off the power. "Look, fellows, I'm just going to put my cards on the table."

"Okay, boss," Jack said as he ran a grimy hand through his graying hair. "If you want to talk things out, I'm ready to listen."

"Me too," Dave said, seating himself on a pile of rope that was lying on the drilling floor.

"Here it is then, short and sweet," Clint told them bitterly. "I've reached the end of my rope. In other words—I'm finished. Through. Washed up."

"But maybe we could drill deeper," Dave offered. "If we go down to another sand, we may hit something worthwhile."

"I think it's worth a try, boss," Jack said from his seat on the driller's stool.

"We can't go any deeper with this old rig, and you both know it. Even at the depth we're at now, it's strained to the breaking point. To try and go down another well . . ." Clint shook his head. "We'd need better equipment. And for that, we'd need more money."

"That's right," Jack said, eager as a bot to keep things rolling. "Lots of people would like to invest in this business."

"Look, fellows," Clint said, carefully weighing his next words in his head before speaking them. "You both know I'm in debt up to my eyebrows. And as of this evening, I haven't got a dime's worth of credit with anybody. My own father told me less than an hour ago that he wouldn't lend me another red cent to sink into the ground. He was my last hope, and he turned me down flat. As I see it, I've only got one thing left to say."

"What's that, boss," they asked in unison.

"My drilling days are over," he said bitterly. "My search for oil has ended. After today, you men will be free of yours truly. Let's hope your next employer will be in better shape financially than I've been. Thanks a million for everything, boys, and the best of luck on your next job."

When he finished speaking, Clint walked to the edge of the rig and sat down on the ends of some casing. Dropping his head into his hands, he thought back to the years the three of them had struggled together. In slightly less than six years, they had drilled twelve dry holes straight. And now number thirteen was ready to be added to the list.

In that moment of dark despair, Clint Johnson likened his search for oil to that of a man searching for the pot of gold at the end of the rainbow. It was bad enough that he had deluded himself into chasing a wild dream over the years, but his men's misplaced faith in him was worse.

Now all they had to show for those years of hard labor was a string of broken promises a mile long and the pitying looks of their friends and relatives. He had failed those who trusted him.

Finally raising his head, Clint looked at the motionless walking beam. An inkling of an idea began to form in the back of his mind. The sand at the bottom of the well was at least twenty feet thick through that section of the country, and Jack had told him he'd drilled into it a little over halfway.

That meant there was still a good six to eight feet of undrilled sand down at the bottom of the hole.

So far the sand had been as dry as a bone. But as he thought on it, Clint became determined to give number thirteen a last chance before declaring it another duster. Old-timers in the oil business had told him of how they had sometimes struck oil right at the very bottom of the last vein of sand they could reach with their outfits. And he suddenly realized that such might be the case with this well.

Springing to his feet, he brought Jack and Dave out of the apathy of defeat they had sunk into with a bellow for action.

"Jack," he said, fixing him with a steely-eyed look. "Didn't you tell me there's still several feet of undrilled sand down at the bottom of this well?"

"That's the way I calculate it, boss. But what's on your mind that's got you steamed up?"

"Simply this," Clint answered, jutting his jaw in determination, "before I accept this well as being another failure, we're going to drill one more screw."

"What's the sense in that?" Dave asked as he built a cigarette. "If the top of the sand's dry, the bottom won't be any different. We've drilled enough wells together to know that. I say you're only kidding yourself, boss." He put the cigarette in his mouth and lit it.

"Dry or not, we're still going to drill one more screw. Even if I have to do it alone. Are you men with me in this last try?"

"All the way," they assured him.

"All right, then. Here's what I want done. Jack, you pull out the tools. We're going to put on the sharp bit. Dave, your job is to see that we have enough steam to cut through the rest of the sand. If there's anything to be found at the bottom of this hole, we'll soon know it."

Within an hour the bit had been changed, the steam was up, and the tools were at the bottom of the hole again. For this last bit of drilling, on what might be the end of his search for oil, Clint Johnson had relieved Jack of his station on the driller's stool.

He slowly let out the screw. As he held onto the vibrating line, he could feel the jar and thud of the drill bit as it chewed its way through the sand deeper and deeper. Overhead, the walking beam creaked and groaned under the tons of weight it was supporting.

Eight more feet to go, he told himself as he fed out the screw. Then there was but five more feet to go, then three, and then only two . . . and then it happened. At the next downward plunge of the tools, he felt the line in his hand go slack.

Clint bent over the yawning mouth of the casing that jutted above the rig floor and listened with straining ears. He heard a faint rumbling come up to him from the depths. When that far-off whisper of sound reached his ears, he felt a tremor run through his long frame.

"Jack! Dave! Close the boiling door. Then come here in the double. Something's happened below."

They raced onto the drilling floor with questioning looks on their grimy faces, and Clint quickly shut off the power and pointed to the yawning mouth of the casing.

Wordlessly, the three of them gathered around it. They listened with bated breath. A moment later they heard a rushing, gurgling roar from far down in the well. Clint sprang backward. "Run for your lives. We've hit something, and she's going to blow."

He grabbed the kerosene lantern from the drilling floor and sped up the little valley that stretched beyond the rig, Jack and Dave following on his heels. When they were a safe distance from the well, Clint blew out the lantern and looked back.

A dark stream of liquid shot out of the mouth of the casing with a hissing roar and cleared the top of the eighty-foot derrick. The watching men could hear it beating against the crown pulley.

Clint raced to the boiler to make sure there was no fire exposed to the gas he could smell. Then he began walking toward the spouting well, keeping his eyes on the stream of liquid.

When the liquid began to spatter his upturned face, he held out a hand and let the liquid collect in his palm. With a quaking heart, he raised his hand to his nose and sniffed the pooling liquid. It was crude oil.

Gazing up at the starlit heavens, Clint Johnson breathed a prayer of thanksgiving as he joyfully wiped the odorous liquid off his face.

"Thanks be to God," he whispered. "My rainbow chasing is over. I've found the pot of gold."

The Enterprising Sheepherder

The late summer sun was a good three hours high that Saturday morning in 1925 when Dan Brooks began arranging the window display of the jewelry store he was managing in Pueblo, Colorado. Engrossed in his work, he paid scant attention to the passersby on the sidewalk outside. And he feared no interruption, because prior to starting the display, he had bolted the street door. Insurance regulations required as such while the display window was being dressed.

Dan carefully placed each piece, employing all the skill he had acquired during his five-plus years of jewelry merchandising in a large eastern city. Before putting the finishing touches on the display, he placed a velvet-lined tray of expensive rings in the forefront of the window, hoping as he did so that the rings would attract the attention of late- summer tourists who might still be in town.

The sharp rapping on the window's glass startled him out of his concentration. He looked up and saw a bewhiskered man of advanced years standing on the sidewalk.

Dan gave the old man a questioning look, and the old man pointed to two of the most expensive diamond rings in the velvet-lined tray and mouthed the words, *How big?* Assuming that the old man was inquiring about the size of the stones in the rings, Dan held up one finger and pointed to the smaller of the two rings, then he held up two fingers with one bent at the second joint and pointed to the larger ring.

By this action, Dan had indicated that one ring had a diamond setting of one carat, and the other ring held a stone with a carat and a half.

The old man smiled slightly and again pointed to the rings while tapping himself on his broad chest. Then bowing in farewell, he turned on his heel and strode off down the street. In bewildered amusement, Dan gazed after the old man's retreating figure. As he did so, he mentally catalogued the old man as a human derelict of the West who was living in a world of his own imagination. The clothing covering his heavy-set figure was old, ragged, and dusty, after all. His pants were patched and tucked into the tops of great leather boots. And a battered Stetson rode atop his thatch of graying, unkempt hair, which stuck out from under the hat in all directions like a small pile of dirty straw.

Dan would have staked a month's wages that the old man hadn't been on speaking terms with a barber in months. "Only a broken-down old bum," he said as he unlocked the store and readied himself for the day's business. "Not a dime to his name, I'll wager, but still he stops to inquire about expensive diamond rings. Honestly. I can't figure a person like that." As the day wore on he gradually dismissed the old man from his mind.

Half an hour before closing time, however, the old man made his second appearance. He strode into the store and greeted Dan with a wave of his heavy right hand. "Evenin', partner," he said casually, a pleasant drawl to his deep voice. "Store still open?"

"I close in thirty minutes, old-timer," Dan replied, giving him a keen-eyed once-over as he spoke. The old man still wore the same heavy leather boots, but new Levi's, plaid shirt, and black Stetson replaced the clothes he had worn that morning. The new clothes improved his appearance considerably, even though his hair and beard were still shaggy and unkempt.

"Good, good," he said. "Now if you ain't got any objections, I'd like a closer look at them two rings I seen in your window this morning."

"Look, sir," Dan said, "I'm quite sure I know what ring you mean, but don't you think that kind of ring is considerably over your head in price?"

"I wouldn't say that, young feller" was the gruff reply. "Whether I buy the *rings* or not is entirely up to me, as I see it. All I want to do right now is look. Any harm in that?"

"None whatsoever," Dan acknowledged. "It's only that I consider it a waste of time for people to look at merchandise that they know they haven't a chance in the world of purchasing."

"Is that the way you've got me pegged, son?" the old man inquired mildly as he stroked his tangled beard.

"Put yourself in my position. The two rings in question are worth *thousands*. And you know just as well as I do that no ordinary person could afford to buy them. See what I mean?"

"Exactly." Then the old man threw back his head and roared with laughter. When his mirth had subsided somewhat, he chuckled. "I know I must look like a dyed-in-the-wool tramp to you, son, but before I leave this store, I'm gonna take a good squint at them there sparklers. So haul 'em out here on the counter, and let's get started. An' another thing. On your way

180

back from getting them rocks, bar the door. I ain't aimin' on bein' interrupted while we're handlin' our little deal. Okay, partner?"

"That's all right with me, old man," Dan agreed dubiously. "But I warn you. Don't try any monkey business. I always keep a gun in the store, and I know how to use it well enough to blow your head off if need be. Understand?"

"Perfectly, young feller." The old man chuckled. "But I ain't lookin' for trouble. Just rings."

Dan bolted the street door and retrieved the tray of rings from the window. He placed the tray on the glass-topped jewelry case, and the old man gazed at them appreciatively for a few moments. Then he asked for a loupe to examine them with.

In increasing wonderment, Dan complied with the request. He then stared in openmouthed amazement as the old man expertly examined several of the more expensive rings. Picking up the two he had inquired about, the old man tried them on and, apparently satisfied, placed the others back in the tray.

"Well now, son," he drawled. "Reckon these two'll have to do. Name your rock-bottom price for both of 'em, an' maybe we'll do business."

"Old-timer, you can't be serious." Dan laughed, amused in spite of his vexation at the absurdity of the request.

"Never more serious in all my living days. If them rings are for sale, an' the price is right, I'll buy 'em both."

"Okay, mister," Dan said, "you asked for it. The price is three thousand five hundred dollars."

"For 'em both?"

"Right."

Picking up the loupe, the old man examined both rings again, turning them this way and that way, so that the diamond setting in each of them seemed to be on fire whenever the light overhead struck the stones at certain angles.

"Wrap 'em up, young feller," he instructed, laying down the loupe. "You just made yourself a sale."

"How about the thirty-five hundred, first," Dan said pointedly. "It's not that I'm doubting your ability to pay, old-timer. Please understand that. But

182

all things considered, I'd like to see some of the folding green before we go any further with this talk of buying diamond rings."

"Fair enough." The old man bent over and pulled off his right boot. Eyeing Dan with twinkling eyes, he reached into the boot and pulled out an insole made of heavy cardboard. This he laid on top of the glass jewelry case. He reached into the boot again . . . and pulled out a thick layer of bills.

Dan stared in bug-eyed disbelief while the old man counted out the bills. Dan could see fifty-dollar bills, hundred-dollar bills, and even thousand-dollar bills in the bundle the old man held in his hand. And when the old man had finished, he still had a sizable handful of bills left, especially the thousand-dollar ones. Because he had given Dan none of these.

As Dan wrapped up the rings and put the money into the safe, the old man carefully placed the remaining bills back inside his boot. Then he put the heavy cardboard insole back on top of them. Pulling the boot on, the old man picked up the packaged rings and bid Dan a cheery "So long, partner." Then he headed to the door.

"Wait, wait," Dan cried as he dashed from behind the counter and ran to the door, beating the old man there. "Look, old-timer, I know I haven't any right to ask questions—especially after the way I practically insulted you—but I can't let you go without some kind of explanation."

"What's wrong, son?" the old man asked, the hint of a smile tugging at his lips. "Ain't my money good?"

"Of course it's good." "Well, what is it then?" "It's you, old-timer." "Me?"

"That's right." Dan gulped.

"See here, young feller, I don't follow you," the old man growled. "Mind explainin' what you mean by that?"

"I'll try my best," Dan promised as he mopped his brow. "Mister, you've really knocked me for a loop, to say the least."

"How come you say that about old Bill?"

"Figure it out for yourself, and put yourself in my shoes while you're at it. This morning you indicated through the window that you were interested in the two rings you just bought. Well, I couldn't believe it then, and I still didn't believe it when you came in a few minutes ago."

"I bought 'em, didn't I? An' paid in cash, too."

"That's right, you did. But I confess I'm still as much in the dark as ever about all this."

The old man chuckled. From the look of him, Dan got the impression that he was enjoying some joke. Finally, the old man said, "Go on, son, only come to the point."

"To be perfectly honest, sir, when I saw you this morning, and again this evening, I would have sworn on a stack of Bibles that you would be the last man in the state of Colorado who could afford to buy such expensive rings."

"By that, young feller, I take it you pegged me for a bum right off the reel. Correct?"

"So help me, it's true," Dan admitted, shamefaced. "But I meant no offense. Please accept my apologies."

"Forget it." The old man laughed. "You ain't the first Eastern greenhorn who's been wrong in his estimation of Bill Dawson. An' I reckon you won't be the last."

"Look . . . Mr. Dawson," Dan said, shaking his head in bewilderment. "I don't mean to sound rude, but you just can't be for real. What in heaven's name does an old-timer like you want with such expensive rings? I tell you, this whole thing's got me buffaloed, as you Westerners say. The rings can't be a present for some woman you've lost your head over as they're both men's rings."

The old man laughed. As he calmed down, he combed his beard with his powerful fingers. "No female has yet got her hooks into yours truly, young feller, an' one ain't about to either."

"What kind of work do you do?" Dan asked. Perhaps by learning about the old man's livelihood, Dan reasoned, he would be able to put the mystery of the man's wealth to rest. He had hesitated to ask the question so bluntly, but on the basis of the man's answers so far, Dan felt justified in simply asking what he wanted to know.

"I'm a sheepherder, son" was the old man's straightforward reply.

"A sheepherder?" Dan mumbled unbelievingly. He was more confused than ever. "And you can afford to buy diamond rings on your wages? No offense, Mr. Dawson, but now I've heard everything."

The old man chuckled. "Son, I reckon I've let my little joke drag on long enough. You don't seem too bad a tenderfoot, so Old Bill's gonna give you the lowdown."

"I was hoping you would," Dan muttered. "So far this whole deal's been over my head. What in the name of all that's holy would a sheepherder want with diamond rings? I tell you, old-timer, it just don't make sense."

"Maybe not to you, young feller. But in the past, diamond rings have made Old Bill plenty of easy dough, and I have a feelin' they'll do it again this fall."

"You mean you make deals with them?"

"I sell 'em for cash." Old Bill grinned.

"But how?" Dan asked. "How can you hope to resell expensive rings and make a profit?" Try as he might, Dan Brooks couldn't accept that this strange old man wasn't pulling his leg. He knew from experience that Westerners were notorious for their practical jokes.

"I've never yet had any trouble resellin' at a profit," Old Bill said with convincing honesty. "As I said before, young feller, I'm a sheepherder. I work on the range out north of Cimarron. I tend the sheep while they're up in the mountains for the summer grazin'. Now here's the deal: Every fall there's

187

always a gang of big stock buyers that come out from Chicago an' St. Louis to buy the sheep that's ready for sale. An' that's when yours truly peddles his rings."

"I don't understand," Dan said while thinking that the whole thing was getting more cockeyed by the minute.

"Simple as fallin' off a log backward," Old Bill insisted. "While I'm showin' them fancy dudes the sheep, I always wear one or more of the rings I've bought ahead of time just for that purpose. An' I always make it a point to see that they spot 'em on my hand. After that, I just sit back an' let nature take its course."

"Go on," Dan prompted with a grin.

"Well, after the dudes eye the sparklers for a while, their curiosity begins workin' overtime an' purty soon they start askin' how I come by the rings. Ha-ha. It pleasures me even now when I think about some of the cock-an'-bull stories I tell 'em. Sometimes I insist the rings come from an old Mexican castle that the Spaniards built. An' other times I swear on my word of honor that I got the rings in a deal I made with some Injuns years ago when I was a young rooster. No matter how I spin the tales, I never fail to insist that the rings are worth a fortune an' that I wouldn't dream of partin' with 'em for nothing short of a barrel of money."

"But surely the stock buyers can tell that the rings are new. One good look would convince them of that."

"Your uncle Bill's too old a dog to be tripped up that way." He laughed.

"Son, after I'm finished workin' the rings over, I swear even the man who made 'em wouldn't know 'em anymore."

"How come?"

"Nothing to it. I scuff, an' scar, an' batter 'em up something awful. Then I polish 'em till they look like they got that way through a lifetime of wearin'. Sort of a trick of the trade. Like agin' likker, only different."

"And you always sell at a profit?"

"Every time," Old Bill said. "I ain't lyin' a bit when I say I've sold many a ring for a thousand dollars more than I paid for it. Not bad for a sheepherder bum, eh, son?"

"I should say not. But look, old-timer, don't you feel ashamed of yourself, selling these rings under false pretenses?"

"Nonsense, boy" was the scoffing reply. "Them stock buyers are out to make sharp deals for the companies they represent. That way they get a rake off. So, while they're doin' their level best to fleece my boss outta his woolies, I'm doin' a bit of fleecing of my own. Kind of balances things out, as I see it." Old Bill walked around Dan to get closer to the door.

"Well, that's one way of looking at it," Dan said, following the old man.

"I calculate it's the only sensible way of dealin' with that kind of skinflint," Old Bill declared. Then he unbolted the door and stepped out onto the sidewalk, Dan following close on his heels. "Son," he drawled, holding out his right hand, "maybe I'll have the pleasure of doin' business with you again sometime. Anyway, I hope so. Got to hit the hay purty soon. I want to make that early passenger for Gunnison in the morning. The buyers will be comin' around in about two weeks, an' yours truly aims on bein' ready an' waitin' when they come. Don't spill my little secret, or I might have to hide out till it's safe to circulate again. Adios."

"So long, old-timer," Dan said with sincerity as he shook the outstretched hand. "Have no fear. Your business secret is safe with me." Old Bill smiled and walked away.

"What a character," Dan said, chuckling. He watched the old sheepherder walk away into the gathering twilight. "To all outward appearances, he's looks like nothing but a broken-down old man with no place to call home except where he hangs his hat. Yet he paid me for those rings with dollar bills, and he still had thousands of dollars left. Just goes to show how deceiving looks can be. And"—he chuckled—"he only pulled off one boot."

A Brush with Death

Did you ever look into one of those big old-fashioned wells that are still common in certain rural districts? And while you were looking down into its dark, gloomy depths, with the water shining from below, did you ever think about what a frightening experience it would be to fall into such a dreadful place?

If you ever have, then read on. I will tell you how such an experience happened to me one cold winter day.

During my early boyhood days, my Father Charles and my Mother Eva, and my four Sisters Hazel, Jewell, Myrtle and Mary and I lived, on more than one occasion, in a friend's log cabin. In fact I was born in such a dwelling.

Anyway, the water supply for such a dwelling sometimes came from a spring that was close by, but more often than not, it came from a well that had been dug deep into the earth until a drip of water was reached. Then that drip welled up, clear to the top.

Usually a wooden border was placed around the top of the well to prevent anyone from falling in. Then a simple wood frame was erected over the well. This wood frame had a spindle, or wooden rod, that spanned the width of the well. A rope would be tied to the middle of the spindle, and a bucket would be tied to the rope. The bucket could be lowered into the well by simply turning the spindle's wooden handle. Likewise, a full bucket of water could be drawn back up by turning the handle in the opposite direction.

Sometimes the wooden borders around the wells were not up to par, speaking from a safety standpoint, which was the case with me and the well I fell into.

On this particular occasion, we lived in an ancient log cabin situated near a low bench by Paw Paw Creek. During the summer we practically lived in this creek. Some marvelous and kindly spirit surely must have kept a watchful eye over us kids in those days. Otherwise we would have drowned, for the water of Paw Paw Creek was way over our heads. And when the creek was in flood, we used to sit in the yard and watch with round-eyed fascination at the varied objects that came floating up. Now, this ancient log cabin derived its drinking and cooking water from a deep flagstone well in the front yard. The wooden border around it was decaying. It was a most unsafe feature where children were concerned.

It was a bitter cold Sabbath day sometime after my fifth birthday in December 1918. A neighbor girl had stopped by to visit. During the conversation that ensued, my father mentioned that he wanted a drink of fresh water from the old well.

So I slipped outside to get my father some water. As I walked to the well, I noticed a thin coating of ice had formed on the stone path leading up to it. I was a child on a mission, so I didn't really think much of it.

When I got to the well, I grabbed the raised bucket in my youthful hands and tugged with all my might to lengthen the rope. Then I sent the bucket whishing toward the bottom of the well. I was leaning against the wooden border around the well, preparing to pull the bucket back up, when the wood cracked. My feet flew out from under me because of the icy stones and I went over the wooden barrier. Down, down, down I fell into the frightening depths far below.

How I survived that fall, I'll never know. Perhaps it was because I had on a heavy fur cap, which incidentally got knocked off on my way down. Then again, perhaps the kindly spirit I mentioned earlier was watching over me. Anyway, I survived.

I hit the water and went down, down. When I surfaced, I had enough presence of mind about me to grasp the rope that was swinging by my side. Placing a foot into the partially filled bucket, I looked up toward the top of the well.

How far it seemed. The jagged sides of the well looked a mile long, and I felt as though I was buried alive.

I was cold, wet, and scared. Blood ran down my face from a cut on my head that I had sustained on the way down. I hung onto the rope and cried, an awful fear clutching my heart.

How am I ever going to get out of here? I thought. *Maybe if I yell as loud as I can,* I told myself, *someone will hear me in the house and come out to see where I've gone.*

So for several minutes I yelled at the top of my lungs. But my voice sounded pitifully weak and ineffective down in the well. Its circular wall of stone seemed to stifle the sound of my cries for help and fling them back in my face.

Worn out by the effort of yelling, I hung my head in despair and gulped air back into my aching lungs.

How long can I hold out? I wondered. I was cold and tired, and in a dim sort of way, I realized that if no one came I would succumb to the cold and my fatigue. I would rest my head on the wet rope, close my eyes, and eventually sink to my death.

As my thoughts reached this low ebb, I heard a shout from above. Looking up, I was overjoyed to see my father looking down at me.

"Are you all right, son?" he asked, seeing that I was holding onto the rope and had one foot in the bucket. "Can you hang in there while I draw you out?"

"I'm falling out," I replied weakly.

Quickly stepping up to the wooden border, my father spread his legs wide and gripped the rope firmly. Then he began to slowly draw me to the top.

The instant he got me to the top and off the rope, he rushed me into the house. At the sight of me, my mother gave a cry and rushed to my side. She helped my father stand me in front of the fireplace before assisting him in stripping me of my wet clothes. When they had ascertained that the cut on my head was the only injury I had, they put clean dry clothes on me and insisted I lie down on a daybed in the living room.

It's wonderful to be out of that terrible well, I thought, as my parents and four sisters hovered over me.

The next morning, as is the way of a strong healthy boy, I was up and about and as lively and full of mischief as ever. None the worse from my fall. My father told me that my oldest sister Hazel was the one who had heard my cries for help and had run inside and told him that I had fallen into the well. She'd been out there looking for a pet tomcat. Her quick work in getting him, and his timely action saved my life.

Now every time I'm down in the hills and I have occasion to draw a bucket of water from a well, I get icy chills up and down my spine as I look down into the well's dark, gloomy depths. *That kind of place*, I tell myself, *could have been where I met my end so many long years ago*. I ponder that ghastly thought, and shudder.

By The Grace of God

The recent tornadoes which swept through southern Michigan, northern Ohio, Massachusetts, and Texas, leaving death and destruction in their wake, recalled to my mind a similar twister which reared its way through southern Ohio more than a score of years ago.

These freakish things which occur in practically every storm such as these are to a large percentage of the people but the singular unexplainable behavior of the storm. While to others, during such a time of stress, whenever lives have been miraculously spared their firm conviction in that this was not accomplished by a freak of the wind, but that these lives were spared in and through the intervention of a Divine Power.

The following story is basically true. In writing it, however, I have permitted my imagination to hold full sway in some respects. This narrative deals with how a young widow, and her two small children, were wondrously passed by when a raging, rearing, whirling cone of death swept over and around the frail shelter they called home one summer afternoon in the late nineteen twenties.

Moreover, aside from the incredible escape from death by the widow and her children, this story relates how a man, who had always doubted the existence of a Higher Power, was brought face to face with an undeniable demonstration of that power. The principals of this story are a poverty stricken widow, her two young children, and a hard shelled stubborn old farmer. The young mother was a devout believer in God. While on the other hand this materialistic, elderly tiller of the soil was one of those rare dwellers of the rural places who never put much stake in anything he couldn't see, or put his hand on.

Barton Powell had lived a long life. And as life had chosen to be hard with him at times, he had never passed up an opportunity to retaliate. This he did by simply returning a like measure of hard treatment, and blows, of one sort or another, to his fellowman for every imagined wrong which came his way. As I said before this man was a firm believer in material things. Always he had considered it a waste of time, and effort, to consume any time on faith in things unseen. Nevertheless, his eyes were opened in a remarkable way that summer afternoon when he witnessed three lives miraculously spared, By The Grace Of God.

Mr. Harold H. Milton

3466 East 119th St.

Cleveland 20, OH

The preachers voice droned on and on. And as his sermon proceeded to grow lengthy the congregation proceeded to grow weary. There was much squirming around by the younger generation, and the adult audience began to show marked signs of restlessness also. But, if Reverend Parson Brown noticed the tired expression on the faces of his congregation he gave it no heed. Because this good expounded of Gods word was wound up like a phonograph. He had chosen the text for his sermon from Christs sermon on the mount, and it delt with people showing kindness and consideration to another.

The church house was a weather beaten edifice situated by a dirt road on a high ridge in a rural district in southern Ohio. It was a hot Sunday morning in early June in the late nineteen twenties. And, as is the way of people who dwell in the countryside, they had come from far and wide to attend Sunday school and to listen to another hells fire and brimstone sermon by the robust ruddy-faced Parson Brown.

Because of the soaring temperature the adults in the congregation were either fanning themselves with pasted board fans advertising a local funeral home or mopping their brows with limp handkerchiefs.

About half way up in the one roomed church house set a man of advanced years. He, too, was a possessor of a square built body, and even though his hair had turned to silver, he still gave to the casual observer the appearance of being as strong as an ox. Barton Powell was indeed a strong man in more ways than one. He was strong physically, strong willed, and also waxed considerable force in the community as a man of financial importance.

Nevertheless, at the moment he presented a picture of extreme disgust. He sat slouched down in the seat by his wife. And instead of giving the preacher his undivided attention he was idly thumbing through an old well-worn song book.

"The weak shall inherit the earth," the droning voice of Reverend Brown cut into Bart's thoughts. At the minister's words the old farmer raised his head and stared contemplating at 3 people sitting directly ahead of him and to the right of him. "Reckon them 3 are the kind that sky pilot Brown is referring to," he muttered. "They sure take the cake when it comes to lack of get-up-and-go. Lack of money too, for that matter." It was the widow Jackson and her two small children whom the well-to-do farmer was staring at with such a disapproving eye. Their features were comely, but the dark eyes of the mother held a deep sadness. Their attire was plain and worn, and patches held the youngsters clothes together in more than one place. They lived on property belonging to Barton Powell for more than 3 years, ever since Mr. Jackson met his untimely death while working on the railroad.

At intervals, he would raise his shaggy-haired head and glare around himself; the while his long scraggly mustache would fairly quiver with indignation. The kindly faced old woman seated by his side paid not the slightest attention to her husbands singular actions. She sat in a dignified composure, quietly listening to the minister. Occasionally her eyes would swing to the right a little and come to rest upon the persons of a young woman and her two children of about school age. At such times her lined face would noticeably soften. And if one would have looked keenly into her tired old eyes then one would have seen tears glistening there.

Eventually Parson Brown brought his lengthy discourse to a close. A song was sung, after which one of the men in the congregation was asked to say a short prayer of dismissal. When this was complied with the services were over.

As soon as the last word has passed the lips of the man who had been chosen to dismiss the audience, Barton Powell hurriedly left his seat and made for the door. However, for all his hurrying to quit the place Parson Brown was there before him. The minister greeted the stern faced, crusty mannered oldster with a kindly word as he held out his hand.

"How do you do, Mr. Powell. How are you this beautiful Sabbath day?" " I'm alright, you hand shaking sky pilot. That is not counting the fact that I'm mad as blazes right now." Old Powell replied in a disgruntled tone of voice. Just then Mrs. Powell walked up to where her husband and the minister were talking. She spoke pleasantly, and as she was shaking hands with the pastor inquired if her husband had been giving out his usual cheerful opinions concerning religion?

"Well now, Mother Powell," Preacher Brown replied heartily. "Bart here was just sounding off again. He tells me he's right angry about something, but I ain't asked him yet what its all about. Reckon though I can guess."

As the minister was talking to the Powells, the congregation came slowly filing out of the church, shaking hands with him as they passed.

Parson Brown laid a hand upon the shoulder of the elderly farmer. A patronizing smile crossed his ruddy features.

"Uncle Bart, as I said before, reckon I know what's riding you," he said slowly in a serious voice. "You can't seem to get that wall of disbelief tore down from around your heart and accept the fact that there is a Divine Personality looking down upon us all at all times. I'm speaking of God Almighty. He is up there Bart, He's been up there from everlasting and will remain for everlasting. Why do you fight that fact so strongly, old Timer?"

"You're right, Brown. Yes-sir-ee." Bart Powell replied doggedly. "All my life, I've been hearing about this Great God that's all over the world. Every since I was old enough to remember anything I've had it pounded into me. How some ever, I still have to say I think its all a great big fairy tale."

"I've always said, and I always will say that if I could see proof of His existence right before my very eyes, I'd be only too happy to believe all this stuff I keep hearing you read every Sunday out of that book called the Bible. How do I know He exists? How do I know this Bible ain't just a perfected story to keep the people in line? I'm an old man, and maybe I'm an old fool to boot, but I believe in things I can see and put my hands on. They're no gain saying the fact that such things exists and are real. On the other hand, whenever you pick up a book and read about something that was supposed to have happened thousands of years ago, I get all peeky feeling inside. There ain't nobody living today that was alive that long ago. Unless, that is, it's this Supreme Being you've been hammering at me about. Well, I've only got one last thing to say. I'm an old Missouri mule, and you've got to show me."

Parson Brown held out his right hand once more to the unbelievable tiller of the soil. A look of quiet resignation settled upon his ruddy countenance as he answered, "Someday, Uncle Bart, I firmly believe the Good Lord above will open these old eyes of yours. There's scales on them, and you can't see what's right under your nose. Saul of Tarsus had the same kind of blindness you're afflicted with, but Jesus of Nazareth took care of that one day on the road to Damascus. I'm not going to try to force God, and His Son Jesus Christ, on you any longer. From this day forward, I'm putting you completely in Their hands. It is up to them from now on. I'll just wait Their pleasure."

"Come, come, now Parson," old Bart hastened to say, "I didn't mean to make you mad. Dog-gone it reckon I've got a right to speak up about what I believe in, and what I don't believe in, same as anybody else."

"Sure you have," the minister acknowledged. "Forget the thought of me being mad at you. I'm not that narrow minded. What I meant was this. The Lord will open your eyes in His own way, and in His own due time. I've got to lock up the church now and be going. I've another sermon to preach in about an hour, and I've got better than twenty miles to go to get there. Be seeing you folks next Lords Day. Cheer up Mother Powell. We'll make a Christian out of this old Missouri mule yet. I'm sure we will if only we can get the Lord on our side."

So, with a hearty laugh, the country preacher, wife, and his 3 children strode to his dilapidated automobile and getting the crank from the floor in the back, cranked the engine till it started running with a roar, and a bang, and a clod of bluish smoke. Then climbing into the car drove away with a dense cloud of dust trailing behind.

The Powells climbed into their fringed topped surrey and with a clucking sound to the fat team of doppled grays began the journey homeward. The horses felt frisky and at times would break into a trot.

Dad Powell I'm right down ashamed to hear you say things like that", his wife burst out. "You've fought the Lord all your life. Only a few minutes ago you were sitting beside me listening to Parson Brown preach and you were ate up with rage and disgusted to see the way people accept without question the existence of God and His Son Jesus Christ. "Why do you act this way? What are you looking for? Are you waiting for a sign from heaven to show you He really exists?"

"Could be right Mother," the silvery haired farmer answered his wife.

In a few minutes, they overtook the young woman and her two children who had also been at church. Old Bart brought the spirited team to a prancing halt, and invited the woman and her children to ride.

"Climb in Mrs. Jackson, why didn't you wait? You knew me and Sarah was going home in a minute or two. I had another little round with that sky pilot Brown about this Supreme Being who's supposed to be running this earthly show. I'm still as unconvinced as ever. Blast it all anyway, he'd be a right sort if only he'd ditch them crazy religious ideas he's always yelling his fool head off about. Is everybody in? Well, git up horses, lets hit the road home."

The ride to the Powell farm was made in less than an hour. A good five miles lay between it and the old church. Going to church from the Powell farm one would have to travel a goodly portion of the distance up the hill, but only on the return trip much better time could be made going down the winding hill road.

About a third of a mile up from his big, white farmhouse, Old Bart drew the team to a halt. A wooded knoll sat on the upper side of the road at this point. Atop the knoll stood a circle of huge maple trees. Nestling beneath the spreading branches of the aged monarchs was a dilapidated two-room shack. At the time of its' construction, this dwelling had been built entirely from unplanned, undried lumber. Large cracks showed between the boards which had been nailed around its sides in what is known as an up-and-down fashion. Only a few cracks had been filled in.

Split shingles served as a roof. They were old and cracked and turned up at the ends. To the casual observer, it would seem that during a hard rainstorm, such a roof would leak like sieve. More often than not, it did. Insecure though the shack was, it served as home for the widow Jackson and her two small children.

The young woman, and her two small children, whom Old Bart had picked up in his surrey on the road back from church, lived there. Thanking him for the lift they climbed out of the vehicle and began walking up a foot path that led up across the knoll from the traveled road.

"Hey, widow," Barton Powell called after her retreating figure. "Don't forget, my rent was due last week."

At his words, Mrs. Jackson stopped climbing the knoll and turned to face her landlord. The children ran up to the little shack.

"I haven't forgotten, sir," she said, with deep anxiety weighing her every word. "You know I always pay on time. It's only that my compensation check is late this month. Soon as it comes in the mail, you'll get your rent."

"See that I do," Old Bart replied. "Otherwise I'll have to ask that you vacate my property."

"But where would I go?" she asked tremulous.

"Fiddlesticks, woman," he snorted unfeelingly, "How do I know or care? I ain't running a free home for widows and their fatherless brats. Got my own troubles."

"All right, Paw, let's go," his patient, long-suffering wife said resignedly. "You've said more than enough for both of us, I'm sure."

"Rags and riches," Old Bart muttered in huge disgust as he drove on. "What a life! By crackly, I'll have my five dollars rent every month from the little house, or that woman and her kids'll hit the road. And I don't mean maybe, either."

With a cluck of his tongue to the horses, Old Bart drove on. When he had drove a little ways he looked at his wife and chuckled out loud. Noticing her husbands mirth the good woman inquired its reason.

"Oh, I was just thinking of something that struck me as funny," he replied evasively.

"Dad Powell was you laughing at that poor widow and her two shabbily dressed children that just got out of our surrey?" Mrs. Powell pursued with a glint of anger in her faded blue eyes. 'Aw, now Sarah, lay off me, can't a man laugh out loud without giving a reason for it?"

"Quit beating around the bush and answer my question, yes or no?"

"Well suppose I was? Is that a crime?"

"No, its not. But ain't that poor woman having enough trouble raising her boy and girl, and keeping them together, without a father and husband to help her, let alone being laughed at? Why do you do such inconsiderate things Barton? Why did you do it?"

"I wasn't laughing at her trouble. Fact of the matter is I feel sorry for her and them kids. There ain't many around here who'd believe that though. But that ain't softening me up any when it comes to collecting the rent for my little house up on the knoll. It's a home for them. And besides that five dollars a month is a return on the time and money I've put into this farm."

"Now look Bart," his wife returned in a disgusted but determined bearing. "You've been hemming and hawing long enough. Why was you amused at Alice and the kids? What's so funny about a poor widow and her children? And I don't want any more of your stalling answers."

"O.K. Mother." He grunted in reply as he swung the horses off the main road and up the graveled driveway which ran up to their house and other buildings.

Their farm was quite large, and fertile one as soil goes. It embraced well over two hundred acres, and lay draped beautifully over high wooded hills and wide fertile valleys. A mile or so up a rather large creek emptied into the Muskingum River to the north of the little village of Lowell, Ohio.

And though in his middle sixties Old Bart, as his neighbors called him, was up early and out late tending his farm. In his community, he was not a well liked person. In fact one would have been safe in saying that Powell was most cordially disliked. He was old, and hard, and cranky. An unscrupulous crafty business man, and a complete and perfect infidel. His was a material outlook on life. As far back as any of his neighbors could remember him, he had never put any stock in things unseen. Another side to his policy of life, which didn't tend to heighten him in the estimation of his neighbors, was his never failing habit of retaliation. Whenever life chose to hand him some hard knocks, Old Bart zealously endeavored to do his best to pass them on. Nevertheless, however, what hard knocks life handed him was far and away ever balanced by good fortune which attended his way.

A big black and white collie dog came bounding and barking down the lane to meet them. As the farmer drew the team to meet them. As the farmer drew the team to a halt by the yard gate chickens and ducks scurried complainingly out of in front of the horses. Before assisting his wife out of the surrey Old Bart looked around towards her with a twisted grin upon his leathery face. Idly he tugged at one corner of his mustache.

"You've been on my neck about why I laughed at Alice Jackson and her kids a while ago. All-right I'll tell you," he growled. "We both know that woman is poor as a church mouse, and badly needs every red cent she can lay her hands on. Well what hits me below the belt is this. Every Sunday, if it's any kind of half-way decent day outside at all she ups and goes traipsing off up that mountain of a hill to that scarecrow of a building you religious folks call a church. And she drags them little kids along, whether it's fit for them to be out of the house or not. But that ain't the half of it. To top that all off every time they pass the collection plate she pulls out money that'd buy food for her and them kids and drops it in the offering. Now tell me. Do you call a thing like that good sense? All that foolish woman is doing is throwing away her hard earned cash on something that don't amount to a hill of beans. When I looked at her climbing the path up to the little house just a few minutes ago it all struck me as being mighty funny. So I laughed about it."

Mrs. Powell looked at her husband and slowly shook her head. Turning to him she laid her hand on his arm in a gesture of deep earnestness. "Dad Powell," she said. "Alice and her children have been here in our property for more than three years now. Every since her husband got killed on the railroad in fact. She's been a wonderful tenant. She's been very nice to both of us. That poor woman ain't got much to get along on. These compensation checks every month ain't half enough and you know it. She's brave, and good, and kind. I'm mighty proud to call her a friend. If she feels she should give something every Sunday; well that's her own business. By the way how much did you drop in the collection plate today?"

"Not a red cent," he replied defiantly.

"And why not," his wife inquired.

"For one reason I didn't have any change. But the main reason I didn't chip in is because I don't believe in it. I can't see any sence in dishing out cash to some mealy-mouthed preacher just because he's handing you a big cock and bull story. And that's that. Come on now and I'll help you out if the surrey. I want to get the team taken care of, and get some dinner. This afternoon I'll be taking a stroll over on the back forty. I've got to see about that flock of sheep."

Mrs. Powell climbed down out of the fringed top surrey, assisted by her husband. When she stood on the ground again the good woman couldn't resist firing a last broadside at her thick headed better-half.

"Barton Powell, reckon I've made up my mind concerning your unbelief the same as Parson Brown has. There just ain't any use talking to an infidel. It'll take the hand of God to open your eyes. I ain't worrying about your soul any longer. When the right time comes He'll know what to do."

Whereupon, after delivering her final shot, Mrs. Powell turned around and opening the yard gate, began walking up the flag-stone walk to her home. Old Bart stood awhile and watched her go, during which time he again commenced tugging at his mustache. Then muttering under his breath the silvery haired farmer climbed back into the surrey and picking up the lines drove on toward the barn and granary, which stood more than a hundred yards beyond the dwelling.

Slowly the long hot days of summer passed by; each new day much the same as the one before. During the weeks that rolled into the past Barton Powell went with his wife to the church house on the hill almost every Sunday. The widow, Mrs. Jackson and her two bright-faced children also were regular attendees. But though Old Bart went quite regularly he did so reluctantly. As if by mutual agreement, since that Sabbath Day in early June, not a member of the little congregation spoke to him of religion, or of God Almighty. This the old farmer accepted as a pleasant and most pleasing surprise. Because it was very annoying for one to have to constantly be on guard in defense of ones convictions. Sometimes the fiery old tiller of the soil wouldn't go inside the church at all. While the services lasted, he would often set in the shade of a rugged old white oak tree which stood in the church house yard. There he would set, an old man, as stubborn and firm in his outlook on life as an old mossy rock. From this vantage point he would rest and day dream, and gaze out over the crests of the rolling Ohio hills.

Parson Brown's attitude towards him was much the same as that of the congregation. If he yearned to make another attempt to penetrate the shell of disbelief encasing Barton Powell heart he gave such yearning no outward expression. Rather it was that he put forth a patronizing tolerance concerning Old Bart, and let it go at that.

The elderly farmer felt sympathetic for the widow Jackson and her two children. But his sympathy never swayed him one penny either way when it came to collecting his rent on the little shack. Then he would be icy-cold and business-like.

"After-all," he had often times told his wife during the three years Mrs. Jackson, and her children had occupied his property, "they ain't my children. It ain't no skin off my nose if sometimes they don't have enough to eat. Now Mother don't look at me that way. I can't be responsible for other peoples offspring. I ain't running a children's home here, you know."

And just as often the good woman would argue with her tight fisted husband to quiet this business of driving hard bargains, to get his eyes open and forget the dollar sign for a while. But though she strove and prayed mightily for her husbands' outlook on life to change, her efforts were fruitless.

The month of June passed into July, which in turn gave way to August. As the hot and humid season drifted slowly by, sharp electrical storms swept over hill and valley. These storms would come sweeping up out of the southwestern sky with s rush and a roar. Accompanied by booming thunder and flashing lightning and torrential downpours.

One Wednesdays afternoon, in mid-August, a bank of clouds appeared on the horizon to the southwest. They were white on top with bluish black undersides. Low mutterings of thunder heralded the approach of another summer shower.

At the first roll of distant thunder, Old Bart and his wife were just settling down to supper, as the storm clouds approached the display of thunder and lightning was unseemly heavy. Although the sun was still two hours high it began to grow ominously dark; with a weird unnatural kind of premature darkness. The country-side took on a weird shadowy cast. Eventually it began to rain. Down it came in a whipping, dashing spray, intermingled with the rush of rain were big hail stones, the size of baseballs. The guest hail began bouncing off the Powell residence with a sharp thud, crash and clatter. A window pane in the front room was knocked into a thousand pieces of splintered glass. By this time Old Bart and his wife had begun to show signs of becoming concerned about the weather. He rose from the supper-table and stepped to the kitchen door. Just then a huge round ball of ice came sailing down out of the stormy sky. It crashed through the upper pane of glass in one of the kitchen windows with a force not unlike a fast thrown rock. Shattered glass flew through the kitchen. With a muttered oath the old farmer stepped out into the yard. Flinging back his silvery haired head he scanned the cloudy heavens with the eagle eyes of one long used to doing such a thing. With a grunt of satisfaction he saw that the cloud formation had broken up overhead. Already the rain was visibly slackening. To the southwest the cloudy sky had taken on a bright pinkish look. With a last glance around he turned around and walked back into the kitchen, satisfied that the unusual summer storm had been but the product of some freakish weather. Already the premature darkness had begun to lift.

Suddenly a new sound fell upon his ears. It came from far across the hills in the exact location from whence the rain and great hail storm had come a few minutes before. At first this new sound was a low far-off rushing sort of roar. This increased in volume rapidly, and seemed to be approaching very swiftly. Again Old Bart scanned the cloud formation to the west. Another blue-black mass of clouds were seen to be pushing their crests above the horizon. As the veteran farmer watched with fascinated eyes this new cloud mass was actually boiling and churning through itself.

With a quick step to the kitchen door, Powell called to his wife. In a moment she stepped out in the yard to stand by her husband's side.

With his thick right arm he pointed to the southwest. Not a word did he say, but just pointed. One look in that direction was enough to tell her the reason for his call.

The bluish-black bank of clouds were pushing up higher and higher.

At the same time, it was traveling towards the old farmer and his wife with the speed of an express train. Sharp gusts of air began to strike them in the face. The roaring, sweeping sound of a moment before had given way to a high pitched whining screech, not unlike the whistle of a freight train. The old couple stood in the yard by the kitchen door, and gazed at the scudding dark clouds before them. Across the little valley from their home rose a lofty wooded ridge. As they gazed in fascination beyond that high timbered rampart, an awful sight met their eyes.

From out of the under part of a huge pillow of the black cloud mass hung a long column. It was shaped like a gigantic cone. And as this terrible formation pushed up and up into their view the kite tail that was hanging out of the clouds was seen to be twisting and turning, round and round in an odd manner, and with a speed that was unbelievable, things were seen to be flying out of this whirling rope of cloud. It topped the timber ridge at which the old farmer and his wife were gazing. The bottom of the whirling cone which hung down to the earth moved a three hundred foot swath through the virgin timber on the ridges crest as if the huge old trees had been nothing more formidable than as many match sticks. Everything in its' path was sucked up and out of sight in the twinkling of an eye. The aged farm couple shook with fear. Clutching each other with shaking hands they huddled down against the outside wall of the kitchen.

The gyrating column of death and destruction swept down the hillside across the valley from the Powell residence. In a twinkling of time the monster of the elements shrieked its' way across the valley directly between the dwelling house and barn. It moved on up the valley in a direct line for the little shack where lived the widow and her two small children.

As soon as the twister had passed by the Powells stepped to the corner of their home and looked in the direction it was traveling. The cloud-rope of death swept on. Gigantic, stupendous, and colossal.

A long sloping spur of hill hid the little shack from view from the Powell front yard. All one could see was the tops of the huge old hard-maple trees which completely encircled the rackly dwelling. With horrified eyes the old farmer and his wife witnessed the shrieking twister engulf the huge strong, old trees. One moment the ago-old giants still reared their proud heads into the sky. The next second they were gone. When she saw this Mrs. Powell turned to her husband, and with a sob in her throat clutched his thick right arm. "Oh Barton," she moaned. "The good Lord above spared our lives, but chose to take the lives of Alice Jackson and her children instead. Right now they're caught up into that awful black, twisting, shrieking thing. They're gone. Poor thing. She had a hard row to hoe." "Now now, Mother," Powell tried to console his wife. "Were still alive, I'm glad to say. For a while I wouldn't have given a counterfeit nickel for our chances. What do you want me to do?"

"If you're still able to travel Pa, I'd appreciate it if you'd go up there an take a look at where the old house used to stand. I'd go along but I'm so shaky I can hardly stand up. It won't do any good I'm sure, but it's the least we can do. Only a miracle from the Good Lord above could have saved her and the children."

"Don't reckon I'd count too much on that." Old Bart replied with a rasp in his voice. "Now that's just what I've been trying to knock into your head all these years. If this God you believe so strongly in really exists, and is so good and merciful, why'd he permit a thing to happen to a helpless woman and two kids like we just saw happen. I tell you it don't add up, or make sense."

"Dad Powell, I ain't in any frame of mind to answer any questions on why this or that is allowed to happen. All I know is that the Scriptures say the ways of the Lord is past finding out. It's not for us to know in this life."

"Find out later. Walk blindly by faith alone. Don't question anything. Just keep stumbling on down life's road. What kind of a religion is that? What kind of a creed is that to live by? I'm sorry Mother if I've always scouted your faith. Show me a sign that He lives, and I'll believe." The old man's voice rang out in sincere derision and unbelief. While they had been talking the elderly couple had gone back into their home. Mrs. Powell took a broom from behind the kitchen door and began to sweep up the scattered glass off of the living room rug. Old Bart went out to the barn to check on the stock.

In a few minutes he returned to report that all is well. By this time the skies had cleared to the west. The sun was nearing the horizon on a faraway ridge clear across the Muskingum River. It seemed to hang motionless in the sky, a great round ball of fire. Already the sky near the horizon had begun to take on ever changing hues. There remained not a trace of the violence of the elements that had raged but a short time before. Now all was quiet, calm and serene. Looking now at this glorious summer sunset one could hardly conceive of the fact that scarcely more than sixty minutes hence death and destruction had come rushing and whirling out of the skies to go marching across the country side.

"Well Mother, reckon I'll be going up to take a look at where the old house stood." Powell informed his wife shortly after he'd returned from the barn. "I tried to use the phone, but the lines are down. I'd like to hear just where that twister came from."

"Only God could answer that question," Mrs. Powell replied from the depth of her favorite rocking chair. "Bart, when you go up the creek and see the spot where our old house use to be, and where Alice and her kids lived, please don't feel badly about it all. The Good Lord above has a purpose behind everything he does."

"Alright Mother, alright, quit your preaching to me" the elderly farmer cut in harshly. "I'm going up right now before it gets dark. And I know sure as shooting I ain't going to like what I find."

With these last few words, Old Bart turned on his heel and walked out of the house. Soon, he gained the public road that ran up and down the valley. Slowly, reluctantly, he began to travel the distance between his home and to where the widow Jackson had dwelled. He walked with his head bowed, his thoughts in turmoil. Again and again, he asked himself the question, why must things like this have to happen? But though he racked his brain trying to find the answer, it eluded him.

When he'd passed the spur of hill that cut off the view of the little old shack from his home, he still walked on with his eyes downcast. Afterwards, he often wondered why he didn't look on top of the knoll ahead. It seemed at the time that a strange power was propelling him on. And he was powerless to do anything but walk. Thus was the manner of his approach to the butt of the knoll.

With dragging steps, he climbed the steep little grade above the road. Every tree and bush that had stood on the sides of this little hill had either been lifted clear out of where they had stood, or had been blown down. Not one remained upright. The white, brown, and reddish roots of trees were turned up to face him on every hand.

At last he stood stop the low valley. As yet, he had not lifted his eyes to look across what once had been a park-like place. What was there to see but death and desolation, he asked himself? But look he must, do with a wrench the old farmer flung up his silvery haired head, and looked out across the little flat.

The sight that met his gaze was one that was destined to completely change his whole outlook on life in the future. There, directly ahead stood the little shack which housed the widow Jackson and her two children. With a rough hand he rubbed his eyes and looked again. Then, to be more positive, he walked closer, but all he saw was something which he had no explanation for.

Not a tree remained standing atop the knoll. And as for the huge old maples, every last one of them were gone, both root and branch. Great ragged gaping holes in the earth was all that remained where once they had stood. Old Bart looked again unbelieving at the little up and down rough-lumber house. At best, it was an unsound dwelling. However, unsound and weak as it was, not a board had been blown off of it.

When the full impact of what he was looking upon impressed itself on his mind, the grey haired old farmer suddenly felt very weak and shaky. The shades of night were falling around him and he was immeasurable grateful for the soft shadows. All at once, he sensed an unseen presence. With a gasping breath he sunk down on the wet earth and desperately wanted to hide himself from it. And bowing his head, he covered his ears with his hands. When he raised his head and looked at the old house again, an oil lamp was burning on the living room stand. He could hear the two innocent Jackson children talking to their mother.

Barton Powells conscience smote him unmercifully as he recalled a favorite verse of his mothers. "James 1:27 : Pure religion and undefiled before God and the Father is this, to visit the fatherless and the widows in their affliction, and to keep himself unspotted from the world."

How oft he scoffed at those words. How oft had he laughed at his mother for her belief in them. But there was naught scoffing or laughter in the heart of Barton Powell that summer evening as he sat upon the little knoll. Rather a great fear possessed his being. In a befogged sort of way he tried to find a natural explanation for why the little house had been spared. After several attempts at this and from every angle, he admitted defeat. Something had transpired here the like of which he had never seen before. Now the truth of those ageless words was indelibly written on his heart for all time and eternity.

What power had stayed the horrible twister from utterly destroying this frail shelter and its occupants? This was the great question which was uppermost now in his heart. But even as he kept asking himself this question, instinctively, he knew the answer. There could be no other explanation. A Divine Power had interceded. Yes, the Lord God Almighty had stretched forth His hand in their hour of need. In that moment of full realization Barton Powell was a soul under conviction. With this thought, the old man began to tremble. How awful was his fear then. Covering his face once more with his calloused hands, he did something which he had always held others in disgust for doing. He prayed. It was by no means an eloquent prayer of supplication. The old mans' prayer was a hoarse, agonized plea for mercy, for forgiveness, for his past unbelief and scoffing, and a humble cry for an opportunity in the future to redeem himself. He felt full realization that he was in the presence of God and became a soul under conviction.

The summer night had shut down completely by the time he rose up from the ground and the little knoll. During the walk homeward, he began to experience a beautiful peace in his heart. All his former doubts and unbelief had fled forever. Parson Brown had been right. His kindly wife also had been right. God, in His infinite wisdom and mercy had chosen a way to reveal His existence. The twister, with its unbelievable power, and destructiveness, had only set the stage for that revelation.

He walked homeward with a buoyancy of step he had not experienced in many a long year. Occasionally he would pause to look long and earnestly into the starlit heavens. At such moments, he would breath a prayer of thankfulness. That day, would forever after, remain the red letter day of his life. A few short hours before, he had witnessed the miraculous escape from sure death of a defenseless widow and her two children. Also, during that same marvelous happening, and as a result of it, he had ceased to be an infidel. Truly it had been a wonderful experience.

As his steps brought him near to his home, his heart became full to overflowing. There, with the stars looking down upon him, and with the night shadows gathered closely around him, he made certain covenants, claiming God Almighty to be his witness.

He resolved from that day forward he would be a stern upholder in the belief of the existence of God Almighty and His Son Jesus Christ. Also, the belief in life after death. No more would he drive hard penny-pinching deals with his fellowman. He'd go to church thereafter, and be thankful for the opportunity. When his thoughts swung to the widow and her children a smile came to his lips. Thereafter they would be more than welcome to abide in the little old house, rent free, for as long as they cared to remain.

That day, he had looked upon strange and wonderful happenings. Instinctively, the old farmer knew that he'd never understand all this.

But deep down in his heart was the unshakable conviction that these things had been made to transpire, only, By The Grace Of God.

THE END

The Phantom of Kinderhook

At twilight the bold thrust of Kinderhook Mountain was outlined against the summer sky in sharp relief. To those looking at the mountain's crest from the east, it always seemed that the evening star was lodged in the topmost branches of the trees growing atop this impressive peak.

Kinderhook Mountain was located about five miles west of the town of Webster Springs in Webster County, West Virginia. The towering landmark soared thousands of feet into the heavens with second-growth timber mantling its rugged outlines from top to bottom.

For many years an air of mystery had shrouded Kinderhook. And there were numerous tall tales about the strange happenings that went on there. Legend had it that in the days of long ago the early West Virginia settlers battled the red man for possession of its fertile slopes. Then after the Indian relinguished his claim to be the mountain the decisive battle between two feuding mountain families had been waged there on. Of late, the local hill folk had added another story to Kinderhook's roster of legendary tales. They claimed that a black snake of unusual length and girth had been seen on the mountain on several occasions. Numerous dogs had chased this snake into the rocky formation of the mountain's western slope and never returned. Full-grown sheep had disappeared, and months- old calves had also come up missing on Kinderhook. The hill folk suspected the snake, but not as much as a trace was left to prove the snake existed, much less that it was responsible for the disappearances.

Then that changed. A lone hunter witnessed the snake in action. The hunter was traveling up a rocky draw that led up to the western ridge. He walked around a large pile of rocks on the ground and ran squarely into the snake. It was busily engaged in preparing a two-month-old calf for swallowing. Before the shocked hunter could recover his wits enough to remember he was carrying a shotgun, the great snake had reared back a good four feet off the ground. It hissed and flicked its forked tongue, then it dropped back down to the ground and disappeared into the rocks that bordered the game trail that ran through the draw.

After that, whenever an animal went missing on Kinderhook, the hill folks knew the snake had just snagged himself a meal. The years passed like this. Animals disappeared, and the lone hunter or two would spot tracks in the dust where the snake had been.

Whether the great serpent had a mate or not, none of the local hill folk knew for certain. They had only ever seen the one snake or a single track at a time. They stoutly maintained, however, that the snake would have a mate. All of God's creatures, they reasoned, paired off that way.

Oftentimes, during the summer months, the young men of the community would organize into groups of four or five and thoroughly comb the rugged terrain of the mountain looking for the great snake and his mate. They searched diligently, but they never found a trace of their quarry.

Eventually interest in the snake's whereabouts waned, and people began to believe that he had died of old age, moved on, or never existed. Soon after, the local hill folk began talking about the great serpent as nothing more than a Kinderhook tall tale. And like most tall tales, the characters in them needed names, names worthy of being remembered. So the local hill folk gave their great serpent a name: the Phantom.

...

From the eastern slope of Kinderhook Mountain, down to the Elk River, there was a sizable valley. And since it was a beautiful spot, Mat Dennis, a stalwart mountaineer, and his comely wife, Rebecca, purchased the valley and several acres of the surrounding mountain slope. They built themselves a cabin on a low bench of the land that overlooked the valley proper.

When the couple moved into their new cabin on the bank of the Elk River, it was just the two of them. But as the years came and went, Mat and Becky had two sons. They named their first son John, and their second Billie.

The Dennis boys grew to manhood in the shadow of Kinderhook Mountain. As mere lads, they would often sit at their father's knee on cold winter nights and listen with shining eyes and quaking hearts to the stirring tales of the violent and adventurous life of the early West Virginia settler. Many and varied were the stories this backwoods father would tell his sons. There were tales of Indian uprisings, Indian massacres, bear hunts, deer hunts, wild turkey hunts, forest fires, terrific storms, fishing trips, and any number of other hair-raising adventures. Whenever their father would tell them about the great snake that had always made Kinderhook Mountain his home, the boys would eagerly listen with bated breath, consuming every thrilling word of the story.

Of all the stories, this one was their favorite. Because, they felt, this one was close to home. Oftentimes as they played along the banks of the Elk during the summers of their early boyhood days, they would pause in their playing and solemnly eye the soaring mountain that rose majestically into the heavens at their backdoor.

"Billie," John would always say then to his younger brother, "when we get big enough to use Pa's shotgun, we'll catch that whopper of a snake he says lives up there on old Kinderhook."

Billie Dennis would look round-eyed at his older brother and nod his tousled head in silent agreement.

As the brothers grew older, they began to wander farther and farther from home while out playing. By the time they were in their early teens, they had explored a goodly portion of the surrounding countryside; they had even ventured onto Kinderhook to explore its vastness. When John turned twelve, their father allowed them to carry firearms while out in the woods. Many were the groundhogs, squirrels, rabbits, hawks, crows, and snakes that succumbed to the blast of the 12-gauge shotgun John carried, or the whip-like crack of the single-shot .22-caliber rifle that Billie always took along on their trips.

The summer of John's fifteenth birthday the boys met the Phantom. It was late August, and, as was the boys' custom on Saturday afternoons in the summertime, they were out groundhog hunting. Luck had attended their efforts that afternoon, and by four o'clock they were trudging home, each laden with a nice fat groundhog.

That day the brothers had chosen to hunt in a section of Kinderhook Mountain that had always been more or less taboo to them, by order of their father. The western slope of the mountain afforded the best possibilities for game of anywhere else on it. It was also the section where the Phantom was known to have made his home in the past.

Knowing this, the brothers had still chosen to ignore their father's order. They had no sooner gotten out of sight of their home, and their mother, when they had thrown discretion to the wind and headed for the western slope. Hours later the brothers started home with the game they had bagged. And unbeknown to them, they had headed up the same rocky draw where a lone hunter had seen the huge snake a decade before.

As the boys neared the center of a cleft in the slope, the two hounds that had accompanied them on their hunt trotted ahead, exploring every nook and cranny of the draw as the boys advanced.

Without warning, the canines set up a great clamor of barking and growling about a hundred yards ahead of the boys. Dropping the groundhogs, the brothers rushed forward to see what had excited the dogs so. Dashing around a bend in the rocky draw, they spied the hounds

leaping excitedly around the base of a huge slab of sandstone that leaned against the side of the draw about fifty yards ahead.

One look in the dogs' direction was sufficient to stop the boys short in their tracks. Their faces turned ashen. There, directly ahead of them, was a huge snake. The snake was at least a dozen feet in length, as thick in the middle as a grown man's thigh, and glossy black in color; and at the moment, it lay draped across the top of the leaning slab of rock around which the dogs were clamoring.

"Oh Lordy, Billie," John gasped as he raised a shaking hand and pointed up the draw, "it's the Phantom, as sure as you're born."

"Shoot him, John, shoot!" Billie Dennis frantically urged in a high-pitched falsetto. "Run up ahead a ways and let drive at him with the 12-gauge."

"But what of the dogs?" John said aghast. "I might cripple one of the dogs for life with this scattergun."

"Hold high then, when you shoot," his brother advised him tensely. "Even if you do nick one of them a little, it's better than letting that telephone-pole of a snake wrap himself around them and crush them to death. Take a good look, John. Can't you see that that black devil is trying to charm them two hounds?"

Billie Dennis had indeed spoken the truth. As John watched the huge snake with fascinated eyes, he could not help but notice that a subtle change had begun to come over the leaping dogs. They were growing

243

quiet, barking and growling only halfheartedly. They also seemed to be growing lethargic.

As John watched, the dogs became as rigid as statues, their eyes never leaving the snake's eyes, not even for a fraction of a second. The uncanny way of the serpent had manifested in a strange and wonderful demonstration of hypnotic power. Then the giant snake came alive.

Slowly, gracefully, he began to glide down the slab of sandstone. His cold, lidless eyes never looked away from the eyes of the hypnotized dogs below. In a ceaseless, fluid motion, the snake lifted his flat head from the surface of the leaning sandstone, his forked tongue flicking in and out, faster and faster.

As though they were in a trance too, the Dennis brothers could only stand and watch the drama unfolding before them. Each knew that something had to be done, and done quickly, or else they would have two dead dogs on their hands very shortly.

When the giant serpent's cold eyes were but scant inches from the big brown eyes of the rigid hounds, the brothers acted to break the spell that the canines were under. With loud yells, they rushed forward. When they were close enough to fire at the snake but miss the dogs, they stopped. John aimed his shotgun at the snake's midsection and discharged it.

The shotgun's violent blast broke the hypnotic spell the hounds were under. No sooner had the blast freed them than the dogs leaped at the snake in snarling fury. But their attack was in vain.

Swift as light, the giant serpent had moved out of harm's way. Gliding up the sandstone slab, he disappeared behind it at the top. The brothers rushed to where the frantic dogs were leaping around and looked earnestly at the huge stone slab from every angle they could view it from. But there was not a trace of the great snake anywhere. He had disappeared.

"Well, Billie," John Dennis said as they stood at the base of the leaning sandstone, "I imagine the Phantom went into that crack in the ledge up there at the top of this leaning rock. No telling how far that crack goes into the mountain. As I see it, there's not much need of us hanging around here any longer. He's gone for sure this time. I'm for hitting the trail for home. How about you?"

Nodding his silent assent, Billie fell into step behind his brother. They retrieved the groundhogs they had shot that afternoon and continued on through the draw and over the mountain in the direction of their home. The long-eared hounds hunted on ahead of the brothers as though nothing of the slightest consequence had happened to them that day.

■■■

Twenty-five months later, almost to the day, the brothers had their second, and final, run-in with the Phantom. Squirrel season had begun in Webster County the Wednesday before. The brothers had decided to forego hunting on opening day in favor of an all-day hunt on the first Saturday of the season.

Their hunting objective that Saturday was to bag the limit of squirrels the law allowed before returning home. So in the cold half-light of an early dawn, they bade their mother farewell for the day and headed for a heavily timbered spur of Kinderhook Mountain that was situated at least five miles to the southwest of their home.

An hour before their father had departed for his daily duties at the huge sawmill in Bergoo. Mat Dennis had worked for the same lumber company for more than twenty years, and he was considered a most trusted and valuable employee.

Good fortune smiled on the hunters that day. High noon found each of them with his lawful quota of squirrels for the day. Coming to a spring of crystal clear water that gushed from a fissure in a tremendous rock outcropping, they decided to stop and eat their lunch. As they ate their simple fare, they congratulated themselves on the success of their hunt. Then Billie said he wanted to start home just as soon as they had eaten and rested awhile. John, however, balked at starting back so soon.

"Look now, Billie," he drawled as he sat down at the foot of a gnarled beech tree that grew close to the bubbling spring. Leaning back against the tree, he regarded his brother thoughtfully, an amused glint flickering deep in his dark eyes. "I know you're itching to get home now that we've got the limit of squirrels for the day. So am I. I've got a date tonight, too, you know. Won't you just stay a little longer and see what happens? We may even find some ginseng.". "It'll do Lola some good to think she's been stood up tonight".

"I'm not staying in these woods until nighttime drives you home. I've got other plans," Billie said stubbornly.

John laughed heartily as he rose from the foot of the tree and stretched lazily. "Stop worrying, please. I want to go sparking tonight, too. It's not like I want to drag around in these woods until the sun sets."

"Maybe not," Billie replied, "but that's not any guarantee to me. I know how well you like to hunt that stuff. If we find any amount at all, it'll be like pulling sound teeth to get you started home. You're like Pa. I honestly believe he'd rather dig ginseng than eat."

"So would I," John said earnestly as they started off from the spring. "But this afternoon, I'll not let my love of hunting it spoil your plans for your night's courtship—or mine, for that matter. Let's hope we round up a nice pile of big roots in two or three hours. Right?"

"Right," Billie agreed.

They hid their squirrels and guns in a hollow log, then looked for sticks they could use to dig up the ginseng. After finding a couple of heavy, hard maple sticks, they set about shaping them for the ginseng hunt ahead. Once done, they headed down the slope to where the vegetation was lush and thick. The hours passed. And with the passage of time, the brothers proceeded to find and dig up a goodly amount of wild ginseng.

Three o'clock found them working out of a tremendous cove that sloped up from the Elk River. Working their way to the right, they eventually came out on the dividing shoulder that sloped down between the cove they had just quitted and the one beyond. A fire had raged there the spring before and much of the younger timber, as well as the mature trees, had been considerably charred at the butts. Numerous saplings had been burned to the point where they had blown down during the summer storms of the past few months.

As they hunted along the burned shoulder, they came to a game trail that ran up and down the slope. Looking down the trail, John espied what he believed was a fire-blackened sapling lying across the trail, some forty yards below.

The brothers slowly worked their way down the shoulder, with Billie hunting about fifty feet above John. Fortunately, the fire had not damaged the roots of the plants they were hunting to any great extent, so they were able to find some beautiful ginseng stalks, which pleased them greatly.

Nearing the place where he had seen what he supposed was a fire-blackened sapling lying across the trail, John was delighted to find it was an exceptionally large stalk of ginseng. As he knelt to dig it up, he heard a slight noise in the leaves behind him. Glancing in that direction, he saw a sight that froze the blood in his veins and caused the hair on his arms to stand on end. Directly behind him, less than a dozen feet away, there was a huge serpent.

The snake was enormous. At least a dozen feet or more in length, and as thick in its midsection as a six-inch stove pipe. At the moment, its head was a good four feet off the ground, staring at something to the side of it. At John's startled movement, the serpent hissed and swung his flat, ugly head in the direction of the mountain youth.

That hiss was the only motivation John Dennis needed to act. With a stentorian yell, he leaped to his feet. "Billie! Come down here at once. I've just scared up the biggest snake that I've ever seen in all my born days."

"Hold everything," Billie answered. "I'll be with you in a second. Maybe it's the Phantom you've run into."

No sooner had the words left his mouth than Billie Dennis was rushing down the mountainside to where his brother stood.

"Wow," he said as he stared at the huge snake with rounded eyes. "How I wish I had a rifle now. We ought to have our heads examined for leaving them in that log with the squirrels. What're we going to do, John? Just stand here and let him crawl away?"

"Absolutely not. If that snake there ain't the Phantom, then it's his mate, or else his twin. As for me, I'm dead set against letting that overgrown bugger crawl away without a fight; gun or no gun."

"John," Billie said, laying a restraining hand on John's shoulder, "promise me that you won't take any unnecessary chances with that snake. If he was to wrap you, he might crush the life plumb out of you before I could get you free of his coils. Just take a good look at the size of that black devil. I'll bet he's longer than a fence rail and thicker in the middle than either of my legs above the knee."

"I don't care if he's as big around in the middle as a hog, and half a mile long," John declared. "I'm going to wade in there and introduce that old boy to this club"—he gripped the hard maple stick tight in his hands—"before I'll be satisfied with this matter either way."

"You're inviting trouble when you get that close to him," Billie cautioned. "One false move and he'd have you in his coils before you could bat an eye."

"Nonsense," John scoffed. "This is a heavy club I'm carrying to dig ginseng with. If I can get a couple of good licks in without any trouble,

250

then I can floor him with this club. Just let me get them in first, and I'll bet my boots that I can put that snake in the ground for keeps."

"But what if you're not able to down him? What then?"

"Keep your pocketknife handy, just in case," John replied quietly as he tucked the club under his arm and then rubbed his work-hardened hands together. He spat on his palms to give himself a better grip on the hard maple club.

"What good would my pocketknife be against a monster like him?" Billie asked incredulously.

"Use it to cut his guts out if he happens to wrap me," John replied as he eyed the nervous snake. Fortunately there were no rocks in the immediate vicinity for the snake to make a dash for. As John continued to eye the snake, the snake dropped to the ground and flattened himself out. The snake attempted to slither away, but letting him slither away undisturbed like that was the furthest thing from John Dennis's thoughts. John took a step toward the snake and waved his heavy club in a menacing manner. The great snake reared back and hissed.

"J-John, be careful. But what good would it do for me to cut him with my pocketknife?" Billie asked. "It would take more than that to do him any real harm."

"I'm not figuring on you killing him with that frog-sticker. They say that a snake loses his strength if you slit his skin with a knife while he's trying to wrap something."

"Let's hope it works if worse comes to worst," Billie said as he eyed the huge black snake apprehensively.

"Okay then," John said determinedly as he got a fresh grip on his club and stepped closer to the swaying serpent. "Here goes, Billie. Stand by now, and keep your head. Don't forget. He's more afraid of us than we are of him. That's for certain."

"Good luck. When you get close enough to reach him with your club, strike like you've never struck before. Do your level best to make that first lick count."

"Right-o." John stepped to within striking distance of the huge serpent. At his approach, the snake became quite belligerent. Omitting another hideous hiss, the snake jutted his flat head forward and kinked his powerful body in a spring-like formation in preparation for battle.

John Dennis wasted no time while his adversary readied for their encounter. With a yell, he stepped forward and swung. The snake jerked violently and swayed, almost toppling to the ground; its lifeblood spattered on the leaves around it. Once, twice, thrice, John swung the heavy maple club as the October sunlight filtered through the trees.

With each devastating blow, the snake's strength and vitality were on display. He seemed indestructible. But the fourth blow . . . the fourth blow sent the huge snake to the ground.

Even then, bloody and beaten, the snake reared back once more and magnificently demonstrated his hatred for all mankind with a hideous hiss, one that was more frightening than all the others. With his wicked jaws wide open, the huge snake made a last supreme effort to close with John. But the terrible beating had taken its toll. The strike the snake launched had but a feeble shadow of his former speed and power behind it and he missed John. The effort taxed him so much that his head sank down on a small mossy rock that protruded above the leaves about two feet in front of him.

At the sight of his momentary advantage, John yelled in triumph and swung the heavy maple club down on the snake's head, crushing it to a bloody pulp. Stepping back then, he and his brother watched in openmouthed fascination as the snake's massive coils knotted and unknotted as death slowly claimed it. John Dennis's face drained of color as he watched the scene before him. He had just realized how easily the life could have been crushed out of him had he been trapped in those coils.

"Well, Billie, that black devil's done for," John said as he removed a huge red bandana from his hip pocket and wiped the cold sweat from his brow with a shaking hand. *Wow*, he thought, *now that it's all over, my knees feel like they are knocking together. I'm as weak as water.* His brother walked around the dying snake and scratched his head in puzzled thought.

"John, do you think that snake there was really the Phantom?"

"Who can say for sure? This old mountain could easily be home to more than one big snake. It's plenty big enough and plenty wild enough."

"You're right, it is," Billie readily agreed. "The snake's dead now. What say we head for home?"

"I'm ready anytime. Boy, I'd like for Pa to see that snake. Maybe we can talk him into coming over here tomorrow afternoon so we can measure this old-timer. My guess is that he'll run more than ten feet," John said as he flung aside his bloody club and started walking up the slope in the direction of their catched squirrels and rifles. His brother fell into step behind him.

···

The following afternoon Mat Dennis accompanied his sons to the spot where the huge snake had been beaten to death. Stretching out the limp body, they measured it. It measured eleven feet, nine inches, from tip to tip.

254

During the years that followed, the Dennis brothers grew to manhood, married, and raised families in the vicinity of Kinderhook Mountain. They never again saw any great snakes, or any signs of one. In time, the brothers came to believe that the great snake John had beaten to death that October afternoon in their boyhood days had indeed been the legendary Phantom.

Pretty Is as Pretty Does

A feeling of anticipation swept through Jasper Stubbins that balmy August morning as he scurried about his apartment. He had overslept, so now he was dashing through some last-minute details before leaving for Hammond's, the department store where he was the sales manager of the fur salon.

"I don't know why," he said on his way downtown thirty minutes later, "but I feel that something wonderful—something exciting—is going to happen to me today. And with a beautiful woman."

Jasper was a bachelor. And he had long considered himself as being quite the ladies' man. His female companions through the years, and there had been many, were of various ages, and all possessed different personalities. Some had been older than him, but many were younger.

Mostly they were sweet, wide-eyed young women with a fervent longing in their hearts to hear wedding bells ring out as they marched Jasper down the aisle. All possessed physical beauty and charm. It pleased Jasper immensely to outwit them and the tender traps they invariably set for him.

"Guess it's my irresistible masculine charm that hooks 'em," he always complimented himself. "That, and my ability to keep 'em in line once they're hooked. This combination never fails to make matching wits with a shapely charmer a most fascinating game."

Arriving at the store, he strutted into the fur salon like a banty rooster and began barking orders to the elderly, dowdy-looking women working under him.

"All right, you debutantes," he said crisply, "look alive. Don't forget, we're starting our annual midsummer clearance today. So for heaven's sake, put some enthusiasm into your sales technique. When the customers begin arriving in answer to our advertisement, be polite and charming. Also, don't just stand around like a bunch of deadheads. Always try to be doing   something   constructive."

"We'll do our best, Stubby," they assured him tiredly as they shuffled about on legs that were as eye-catching as so many fence posts.

"That's another thing, girls," Jasper said, his black eyes flashing angrily behind his horn-rimmed glasses. "This habit you've fallen into of addressing me as 'Stubby' has got to stop. Kindly remember that from now on I am to be addressed only as Mr. Stubbins. Understand?"

"Yes, boss," Maggie Phillips said, smiling. Then she went about her task of tidying up the salon for the day's business. "Mind if I make a suggestion?" she said, not looking at Jasper.

"Not at all. What is it?"

"Perhaps if you'd loosen up a bit and marry one of those glamor queens you're always chasing, your temper would improve. I think it's worth a try. Don't you?"

"Never," Jasper snorted, giving his thinning hair a smoothing pat. "Courting beautiful women is a fascinating game for me. But that's as far as it goes. I prefer to leave the marrying of them to the suckers. The gal hasn't been born yet that can take your uncle Jasper for a ride. Their intentions are much too obvious right from the start. Be on your toes today, Maggie. There's work ahead."

"Anything you say," she replied, shuffling away.

As the morning dragged by, the response to the advertisement concerning the price-cutting sale on expensive fur coats did not materialize

259

as Jasper had hoped. In fact, less than a score of customers had come in to investigate the possibilities of a bargain. Those who had, well, the greater percentage had been elderly wives and mothers who had patronized the store before.

It disgusted him immeasurably to watch them trying to squeeze their pudgy bodies into coats that were several sizes too small for them.

"Gad," he muttered, watching them twist and turn from the privacy of his office. "What a prize-winning flock of old hens to be cooped up with. If my transfer to men's clothing doesn't come through soon, I honestly believe I'll go batty. That feeling I had earlier today was probably a false alarm."

The other customers that came in response to the ad were lovely young things that had also been in the store before. But instead of being wives and mothers, they were members of that group of young women who had lowered the standards of their conventional upbringings to become mistresses of rich, elderly husbands and marriage-wary bachelors.

They were also accompanied by these hawk-eyed men of the world. And their attentiveness and watch-dog airs spoke plainer than words that these men considered the delectable feminine dish they were spending their hard-earned cash on as their own personal property. To invade the privacy of such a setup, Jasper had learned from previous experience, was an invitation to trouble.

As he stood and watched the women pawing over the merchandise and haggling over the prices, he fervently wished for a young, beautiful, *unaccompanied* customer. One that would lift his sagging spirits and make the boring position he occupied bearable.

"A little excitement and intrigue with a woman today would be like a shot in the arm," he muttered. "The way I feel now, I'd be tempted to give a week's pay for the privilege of serving such a dame."

Just then the drapes separating the fur salon from women's lingerie parted. A honey blonde stepped through. She was young, with a doll face and a figure like a cuddly kitten. She paused on the threshold a moment and swept the room with a pair of big blue eyes that were as innocent and inquisitive as a baby's.

When Jasper realized she was alone, he threw discretion to the wind and dashed forward, unceremoniously brushing one of the sales ladies out of his way in his mad dash to reach the young woman's side. He was determined to wait on this lovely creature himself.

"May I help you, Miss?" he inquired in his best professional voice and manner.

"Hello there," she said breathlessly, flashing him a dimpled smile that would have done credit to a movie queen. "Gosh, oh me, I hope so."

"What did you have in mind?" Jasper asked, delighted at the helplessness she radiated.

"Why, a fur coat, I guess. I saw your ad in this morning's paper."

"Then please step right over here to your left," he graciously invited. Moving to one side, he waved her on ahead of him. As she wiggly-walked past, he joyfully feasted his eyes on her full, rounded breasts, which fought against the confines of her low-cut blouse. Then he shifted his appraising scrutiny to her incredibly slender waist; then her beautifully contoured hips; and then her shapely legs, which her tailored skirt enhanced most intriguingly.

What a babe, he thought. *And lost in the woods to boot. How about that for luck? Daddy Stubbins is just the man to steer this lovely little lady right.*

"And now, young woman," he said, walking past her to slide open the glass-paneled doors of a huge coat case that occupied the entire wall of one side of the room, "just take your pick. These are our better coats. Before you hangs the largest selection of fine fur coats this town has to offer."

"Oh, aren't they just darling?" she said, hurrying forward on her high-heeled pumps. She began running her hands lovingly over the sheer beauty of several of the garments.

"See anything you like among that lot?" Jasper asked. But even as he voiced the question, he knew it was a needless one. She was flitting from coat, to coat, as happy as a child at an ice-cream party.

"I love them all."

"Of course you do." He laughed. His head was whirling from the breathless way she talked and the sweet smell of her perfume as she clutched his arm in her excitement over the coats. "But isn't there one that you like better than the others?"

"You've guessed it." She dimpled, showing just the tip of her pink little tongue between her white, even teeth. "That's why I like doing business with an older man, like you. It just seems natural for you to know, even without asking, what a girl like me wants, and needs, the most."

At her honeyed compliment, Jasper's chest visibly expanded. Smiling smugly, he patiently waited for her to point to a coat she wanted to try on. After a moment, she pointed to the coat of Persian lamb.

"May I try that one on?" she asked.

"You certainly may," he replied, stepping to the coat indicated. He removed it from the hanger and held it open for her. With a little-girl exclamation of joy, she quickly slipped into the garment. The coat was a beauty. And when she pivoted before a full-length mirror, it swirled about her trim figure in soft, luxurious folds.

"How do I look?" she asked, her beautiful features all flushed and happy.

"Wonderful," he assured her. "But you're the type of girl that would look positively ravishing in anything . . . or nothing," he added daringly.

She blushed prettily. Then she pushed the coat collar up around her face and regarded him flirtatiously with her big blue eyes.

"Oh you—you big, bold man, you." She giggled. "It's like mother's always telling me. All you worldly men just love to look at females in the nude, now don't you?"

"Only a dead man would pass up looking at a lovely girl like you, you dear," Jasper said. "And I do mean 'look.' At anything we can see. Anytime. Any place. Any way."

"Thank you, thank you, kind sir." She laughed, taking another whirling step before the mirror. "You're naughty, but awfully nice and exciting to be around. Too bad I'm so young and inexperienced with men. 'Cause it'd be simply peachy to get to know you lots and lots better. But it's just my luck to be stuck with a narrow-minded man for a father."

"Parents can be a problem, sometimes," he sympathized.

"Anyhow, my father probably wouldn't be the only one that would stand in the way of you and me kicking up our heels. What about your wife?"

264

At her roundabout inquiry as to his marital status, Jasper smiled inwardly. In that moment, he was proud that he was a bachelor and hastened to tell her so.

"Whoa there, little girl." He laughed. "Have no fear of a wife, as far as I'm concerned. Before you stands an unattached male. I have no wife, and never have."

"I'm not in the least surprised," she murmured, her big blue eyes regarding him most appreciatively. "Married men have a look about them that a discerning girl can spot a mile away. They seem to be bound down, or something. And their looks and actions show it."

"I know what you mean. I've noticed it too. Poor devils."

"That moment I saw you today, your appearance impressed me very different than most men's. Somehow or other your every word and action fairly screamed that you were—well, unfettered. I like that in a man."

"Smart girl." Jasper applauded. "All beautiful girls, like you, have beautiful eyes. I'm sad to say, though, that too few of them know how to analyze what they see. I'm so happy to learn you aren't one of those females. Something like that always makes a man feel real good."

"You're awfully nice, and kind," she murmured with downcast eyes. "But I don't know your name. Mine's Dolly James. What's yours?"

"Please forgive me. I'm very sorry for being so thoughtless. You see, Dolly, most customers don't give a hang about the salesperson who waits on them. It really brightens a person's outlook on life to meet someone who looks at things differently. My name is Jasper Stubbins. And it is a pleasure to make your acquaintance."

"You have a very nice name," she said. "So masculine and commanding sounding. It fits you."

Again Jasper's chest threatened to pop off his shirt buttons. Many a long day had passed since he had waited on such a beautiful, forthright customer, and he was enjoying himself to the fullest.

During the next half hour, Dolly James tried on every fur coat in her size in the salon. There were so many darling ones, she told Jasper repeatedly, that she was lost as to which one to choose. At last, after many breathless oohs and aaahs, she narrowed her preference down to two. One was the first coat she had tried on; a Persian lamb valued at six hundred dollars. The other was an exquisite muskrat creation priced at four hundred dollars.

While she was striving to make her selection, Jasper was able to learn numerous things about the lovely young Dolly James. She was but twenty-one, she assured him solemnly. And she was unmarried.

Unfortunately, her parents had badgered her into becoming engaged that summer to a young man who was an old friend of the family.

"Hubert's all right, I suppose," she murmured. She slipped into the muskrat coat again and admired herself in the full-length mirror. "It's only that he's so dull and backward, if you know what I mean."

"I understand." Jasper nodded, happy that he was no longer in the young and inexperienced stage of life.

"Us modern girls prefer men who aren't slow about taking the initiative in certain . . . delicate matters . . . that are of vital importance to the development of our personalities. It's a known fact that every girl needs a well-developed personality. All noteworthy psychologists agree on that point. Don't you, Jasper?"

"Emphatically." He smiled. "I feel that it's up to us men to see you get it too. It would be nothing short of sacrilege for a sweet young woman like yourself to throw herself away on a dolt who wouldn't appreciate her many charms . . . and hidden beauty too personal to mention."

"Ah, I just knew you would understand," she breathed. "Too bad I'm only visiting relatives here in a town for a week or ten days. It'd be ever so exciting, and educational, to learn more about the facts of life with a man like you to teach me. Wouldn't it be fascinatingly wicked to put Hubert out of my mind for a few days and sort of live it up—recklessly?"

"It would be the most exciting and wonderful experience of your young life," Jasper whispered hoarsely into one of her pink little ears.

As he gazed at her luscious figure, he recalled the many love trysts he had had with passion-ridden women in the past. His bachelor apartment was the scene of numerous such meetings, as too were hotel rooms.

Dolly James seemed to him like a young woman who would be gullible to flattery. Her eager, excited way of talking and acting proclaimed this fact as surely as if she had shouted it from the rooftops.

With this knowledge, Jasper began formulating his plan of conquest. His paramount desire was to completely possess her sweet, young loveliness through wild, passionate lovemaking in the privacy of his apartment.

This babe is actually begging for a man to teach her about the birds and bees, he thought, drinking in the picture of feminine loveliness she presented. *If I play my cards right, perhaps Uncle Jasper can accommodate her in that respect.*

"Oh, I'm sorry for being such a nuisance." She interrupted his thoughts. "I just know I'm wasting your valuable time. I just can't seem to make up my mind as to which of these two beautiful coats I should buy."

"Dear lady," Jasper said, smiling reassuringly, "please feel free to take as long as you wish to decide. After all, you're the one who'll be wearing the coat. And I feel obligated to tell you that a more beautiful young woman couldn't possibly be making the decision."

"Thank you, so much," she murmured, flashing him another one of her dazzling smiles. "Now, Jasper, just so you know, I'm serious about purchasing a fur coat. I'll be paying for it with this bill Daddy gave me when I started downtown today."

Opening her expensive alligator-leather purse, she drew forth a small silken coin purse. Unzipping it, she took out a folded bill. This she handed to Jasper with an air of supreme confidence.

"Here's the loot, as my daddy always calls money," she said. "He suggested that I have the store check it. That way we'll all be safe and satisfied. Right?"

"Great day in the morning." Jasper whistled, looking bug-eyed at the one-thousand-dollar bill she had handed him. "Dolly, I'd say you're one fortunate girl to have a father who's able, and willing, to be so generous with his children."

"Daddy's a peach that way. But he can afford it."

"What does your father do for a livelihood?"

"He makes things," she said. "He's got a plant, or factory, on the west side of town where we live. And, anyway, I'm an only child."

"I see," Jasper said, his mind racing a mile a minute. "Now you sit tight and I'll be back in a jiffy. The bank's right across the street. Checking the genuineness of this bill won't take long."

This chick gets more interesting by the minute, Jasper thought as he turned and left for the bank. *She's not only as pretty as a picture and as innocent of the ways of men as a mere child, but she's also filthy rich. Man, oh man, what a prize for the picking. Too bad I'm twice her age and she's only visiting in town. Oh well. I'll still be able to pop her corn if I play my hand right. At least I'm going to try.*

Ten minutes later, he was back in the fur salon, a big smile on his face.

"My dear girl," he said, beaming, "your money's as good as gold. Now tell me which coat you've decided on. I'll be more than happy to wrap it up for you and give you your change."

"I feel positively awful," she cried, rubbing her smooth forehead in a gesture of absolute mental distress. "Even after all the trouble I've put you to, I'm still not sure. Tell you what"—a sudden bright smile flashed across her beautiful face—"I know this sounds terrible, but I think I should shop the other stores in this area before I decide. Even with the indulgent father I've got, I don't do this sort of thing every day. I promise that if I don't find anything in the other stores I like better, I'll be back later today and take one of these two coats I'm undecided about. Fair enough, Jasper honey?"

"Why certainly, Dolly," he assured her. "Your complete satisfaction is of prime importance to us here at the store. Take all the time you want to decide. I'll be right here to serve you when you return. I feel positive you'll be back. Anyone can tell you that Hammond's has the finest selection of fur coats in town."

"You're a living doll," she breathed, stepping close. She batted her big blue eyes up at him in an intimate sort of way. "But please don't look heartsick. I only want to look in the other stores. It's more to give myself time than anything else. I'd be willing to bet that I'll be back here again in less than two hours. Being a woman, I can't bring myself to grab the first thing that catches my eye. Understand?"

"Perfectly." Jasper smiled broadly. "What you propose is perfectly normal. Ninety-five percent of our customers always shop the other stores before consummating any purchase with us. Here's your money, Dolly. Look carefully before you buy any expensive item." He sighed, frowning. "I hate to see you go. Once you step out of this salon you'll step out of my life forever. It's a shame. And just when we were getting so well acquainted. Why it's—"

"Oh hush kind sir," she said, laying a soft, cool hand across his mouth. "This isn't the end of the world. If it'll make you feel better, I'll stop in to say good-bye before I leave for home. People may call me an old softie, but I just can't bear to hurt any of my friends' feelings."

"Of course you can't. Now be sure you keep your promise. I'll be depending on you."

She smiled up at him shyly. Then she returned the money to her purse and walked away, glancing back briefly to wave good-bye.

•••

The day wore on, and closing time drew near. When only twenty minutes remained until closing, the drapes leading into women's lingerie parted and Dolly walked through.

At the sight of her, Jasper rushed forward and greeted her with a broad smile and outstretched hands.

"Welcome back," he said joyfully. "Honestly, Dolly, since you left, I've felt lower than a snake's belly. I know that's a very ungentlemanly thing to say to a fine young woman like yourself, but I feel I must be honest."

"I understand." She smiled, a little misty-eyed. "As I said before, I'm an old softie too. I've come back to purchase the Persian lamb coat. You were so awfully nice that I feel it's no more than right that you should make a sale. Here's my money again. I'm sorrier than I can say that our friendship has to be so short. I just know we could find oodles and *oodles* of fascinating things to do together if only we could have had the time and opportunity to know each other better. Don't you think so too, Jasper honey?"

"I'm sure we could," Jasper agreed, handing her the wrapped up coat and four hundred dollars in change. "Look, Dolly, what about alterations? Perhaps you better give me a phone number where I can reach you in a day or so. Hammond's wants you to be perfectly satisfied with your new coat, you know."

"Silly man." She dimpled. "You know perfectly well this coat's just the ticket for little old me. I love it. But," she added, laughingly, "if it'll make you feel any happier, you can reach me at Skyway. Here's the number"—she wrote it down and handed it to Jasper with a shy smile— "Perhaps we could have lunch together or do something exciting before Daddy and Mother carry me back home to Hubert. Okay?"

"Wonderful," Jasper said, pocketing the number. He extended his right hand to her. "Bye-bye, Dolly. I'll phone you tomorrow."

She flushed prettily as she removed her glove and slipped her hand into his outstretched one.

"Please don't ring me too early. I'm an old sleepyhead, and I'm not fully awake before ten AM."

"I'll remember that when I call. Oh"—he gripped her hand and smiled sheepishly like he'd just thought of something—"why not let me drive you to wherever you're staying? It's closing time, and my car is parked right behind the store. As soon as I lock up here, we can be on our way."

"I'd love that, Jasper honey, but I really shouldn't," she said, pulling

273

her hand away from his.

"Why not?"

"It's my daddy. Since I agreed to the engagement, he's been behaving like a watch dog where I'm concerned. He acts like I'm going to run off and marry some other man. You see, Hubert's folks have an awful lot of money. He's an only child, same as me. I guess they plan to cement the families' fortunes through our marriage. Aren't parents silly that way?"

"I understand." He smiled. "But keep your chin up. You may outwit them yet and marry a man of your own choosing. There's many a slip, you know."

"Maybe, but it's not likely." She sighed and repositioned the packaged coat in her arms. "Bye-bye, Jasper honey. Daddy's meeting me in the square in ten minutes. I've got to hotfoot it, or he'll be kept waiting and I'll get a scolding. Bye, again, I'll be expecting your call tomorrow. Make it at eleven."

"I'll be counting the minutes till then."

Pivoting on her heel, she walked across the salon, her beautifully rounded hips swaying rhythmically with every step. She paused a moment at the draped entrance and turned. She flashed Jasper one of her dazzling, intimate smiles. Then she waved good-bye, stepped across the threshold, and was gone.

■■■

The following morning Jasper launched himself into the day's work with more zest than he had evidenced in many months.

"Life," he mused, watching the clock, "can still be plenty exciting and satisfying, even for a man of my age. Provided one but takes advantage of the opportunities that come one's way."

At eleven sharp, he hurried into his office and dialed the number Dolly had given him. A recorded announcement said that the number he had dialed was not a working number. He shook his head in perplexity and repeated the operation. Again, the same announcement came over the wire. More perplexed than ever, Jasper hung up.

"Perhaps," he muttered, "when I don't call at the pre-arranged time, she'll realize she gave me the wrong number and phone the store."

■■■

Lunchtime came and went. And still no call came in from Dolly. By then Jasper didn't know what to think. At half past one, his phone jangled. Dashing to it, he grabbed it off the hook and said hello, his voice carefully modulated.

A crackling order came over the wire. Jasper's sudden flare of expectation sank like a leaden weight. It was the president of the store summoning him to his office on the fifth floor, immediately.

On his way upstairs, he recalled that Mr. Howard's voice had sounded curter than usual, but Jasper dismissed it on the grounds of the man's atrocious temper. *Perhaps my transfer to men's clothing has been approved*, he thought. *He's probably just put out at having to replace me in the fur salon.*

When he reached the frosted glass door of the president's office, he paused to straighten his tie. Then he squared his shoulders and knocked.

"Enter."

He pasted a smile on his face, opened the door, and walked in.

At the dark look on his superior's face, Jasper became uneasy. He approached the desk cautiously, praying he was about to hear the news of his transfer and not something else.

"Stubbins, you're an idiot," Clement Howard greeted him, his steel-gray eyes flashing fire.

"An idiot? *Me.* I don't understand."

"Let me enlighten you then." Howard opened a drawer in his desk and withdrew an envelope. He extended it to Jasper.

"Look inside. Perhaps its contents will throw some light on my most recent observation of your mental capacities."

276

It's an approval for my transfer to men's clothing, Jasper thought as he accepted the envelope and withdrew its contents. One look at the paper in his hand, however, threw him into a complete tizzy. It was a one-thousand-dollar bill.

"I-I-I . . . It's a mistake. This can't be the same money I received in payment for a Persian lamb coat I sold yesterday afternoon."

"Oh, but it is, Stubby old boy."

"I can't believe it. She was overjoyed with the coat when I sold it to her. And now she wants her money back. Is that it?"

"You tell me," President Howard growled.

"Look boss," Jasper said, his composure fast returning. "Let me handle this. I'm positive I can convince her that that Persian lamb coat is just what the doctor ordered. Think no more about it. She and I are supposed to have a talk today. Just leave everything to me."

"Come off it!" Howard snapped. "For once in your life, get your big feet on the ground and that balding head of yours out of the clouds. Your little blue-eyed darling still loves the Persian lamb. I'm quite sure of that. It's the bogus money she paid for it with that's got my dandruff up."

"Impossible," Jasper gasped. "Mr. Howard, this bill's got to be genuine. I took it over to the bank myself to have it checked. It was as good as gold."

"I'm sure it was, but this is not the same bill."

277

"But it's got to be."

"Convince yourself, then." The store president pointed to the envelope. "There's a note in that envelope you're holding. Take a look at it. The bank sent it back with the bogus bill."

With shaking hands, Jasper withdrew a pink slip of paper. He had overlooked it when he had removed the one-thousand-dollar bill. Fearfully he turned it over—and sustained a violent shock. The word "counterfeit" was stamped on the paper in big, bold, black letters. Under the word, he vaguely recognized that there were three or four lines of text in smaller type. But all Jasper could really see in that moment was that one condemning word—**COUNTERFEIT**.

Wiping the cold sweat from his brow, he lifted an ashen face to his superior.

"Surely there's some mistake," he whispered. His faith in his ability to judge women was completely shattered. "Boss, I would have staked my life on that girl's honesty. She was so young, and pretty, and innocent, and—"

"Innocent, my foot." Clement Howard snorted in disgust. "Young and pretty, yes. But that little lady was experienced enough to pull as slick a con game on you as you'll ever see."

"What happened?" Jasper mumbled, sinking into a chair. "Somehow I still can't believe all this."

"Let's face it, Stubby," the old man growled. "You've been taken. From what I hear, it's no wonder though. The way the girls of the department describe it, you were drooling like a hound from the moment that chick walked into the fur salon."

"Why, why—I was only trying to make a sale." Jasper gulped, his face turning red, then white, by turns.

"Exactly." President Howard laughed. "But if I know you, it wasn't fur coats you were trying to push. In fact, I'd be willing to lay anyone odds that your mind jumped into the gutter the instant you clapped eyes on that babe."

"But I-I-I meant her no harm," Jasper said, red faced. "She asked me if there were any interesting things I could show her—sexually. Her utter helplessness was an open invitation to any man that she was a pushover."

"All part of an act to throw you off your guard. Then, when she asked for the opportunity to shop the other stores before making up her mind, she set up the perfect way to switch the good bill for the bogus one. She also made it a point to come back to the store after the bank had closed for the day. That way she knew you hadn't a Chinaman's chance of having the bill checked again before this morning. And you fell for the switch: hook, line, and sinker."

"Boss," Jasper groaned, "I so let you down. I don't know what to say."

"I can imagine that."

"It's a dirty shame the store got fleeced that way."

"Guess again, Stubby old man," Clement Howard said, his voice as brittle as thin ice.

"I-I-I don't understand." Jasper gulped.

"This was your deal from start to finish," the store president said coldly. "And I hold you personally responsible for the loss."

"A thousand dollars," Jasper gasped. "My savings will be practically wiped out. Boss, I won't take this lying down. No, sir, I won't. No woman can play me for a sucker like she did and get away with it scot-free. I'll put the law on her trail within the hour. That little lady will be taught a lesson she won't forget in a hurry."

Leaping out of his chair, Jasper made a mad dash for the office door. But at the bulldog like roar from his superior, he paused.

"Sit down, you blockhead," Clement Howard shouted. "Now get this straight. I will fire you before I will permit you to go off all half-cocked and involve the store in a legal merry-go-round. For heaven's sake, use your head for once in your life. Can't you see? To order that girl's arrest would be to lay ourselves wide open to a honey of a false-arrest lawsuit. Not to mention defamation of character and other legal action she could bring against us. I say forget it."

280

"But she cheated us out of a thousand dollars," Jasper said angrily as he reseated himself. "And you're saying forget it. Boss, either you're off your rocker, or my ears are playing tricks on me. I'm all confused."

"Then I'll spell it out for you in words of one syllable. Correct me if you still think I'm off my rocker after I've had my say."

Jasper nodded.

"Now then, the first bill she gave you to have the bank check was as good as gold. Right?"

"Right."

"Good. When she came back to the store, she gave you what you thought was the same bill you had the bank check. Yes?"

"Yes," Jasper said weakly.

"Please tell me this, then: Do you think for a pair of American minutes that you could prove in a court of law that it wasn't the same bill?"

"I-I-I don't know if I could or not."

"Exactly. Now you're beginning to get the picture. The judge would take one good look at that blonde doll-baby and laugh you right out of the courtroom. Be sensible, Stubby. The risk involved in having her arrested is too great. It's better this way."

"But what about my thousand dollars?" Jasper wailed.

"Chalk it up to experience," the store president snapped. "Don't forget, it could've been worse. Let this be a lesson to you. Next time a sweet, innocent-appearing young thing walks in, let one of the sales girls in the department handle her. Play it safe. Maggie and the other girls can spot a phony a country mile away."

"I still think the law should be notified of this swindle," Jasper said, crossing his arms over his chest.

"And get ourselves involved in a beautiful batch of unfavorable publicity? No thanks. As I said before, I'll dispense with your services here at Hammond's rather than sanction any such action."

"Boss, are you sure you couldn't let the store absorb this loss?" Jasper ventured.

"Not a chance." President Howard pushed back his chair and got to his feet, silently indicating that the conversation was over. "But I will make this concession. You can settle for the loss of the coat at wholesale. Good day, Mr. Stubbins. In the future, while you're on the job, tend strictly to business. And I don't mean monkey business. Should you desire to feast your eyes on a pretty face and a wiggly posterior, I suggest you take in a burlesque show. It'll be far easier on your pocketbook in the long run."

···

What a fool I was, Jasper silently upbraided himself on his way back down to the fur salon. *It really serves me right, though. With all my experience, I should have remembered to never underestimate the ability a beautiful woman has to deceive. Anticipation? Bah. Next time I'll listen to my commonsense, and not some foolish fancy. If the girls in the department hear of this, I'll never live it down. Couldn't blame 'em much for razzing me about it either. Gad I sure asked for this trip to the cleaners.*

Gathering Ginseng and Goldenseal For Pleasure

About the author

Harold H. Milton.

I was born in a little log cabin in Southern Ohio, east of Marietta on December 23rd, 1913. My early life in the hills and hollow of that part of Washington Country in Ohio were spent in fishing and frog hunting in summer, also roaming the woods with my, Father Charles Henry Milton, born 1872 in February and passing away November 1946. I was always happy when I became old enough to go with him. My Mother is Eva Marilla Farley Milton, born January 6th 1885. Together with going to a one room school house from September to May, and hunting and running a trap line in winter at an early age, my father taught me to hunt Ginseng and Yellowroot. Also, he taught me the names and how to identify a host of other herbs. For this teacher and the knowledge he departed to me in my early life, I have always been very thankful.

I graduated from the 8th grade of school in 1930. That ended my formal schooling. At the time, the big depression was on, full sway. Jobs were practically nonexistent. Literally hundreds of thousands of people were traveling from one end of the country to the other looking for work. Fortunately, it was that my Fathers knowledge of the woods and herbs therein were put to good use.

Prices for dry herbs per pound fell to an unbelievable low. My father and I sold dry wild Ginseng root during the early 1930's for less than $5.00 a pound. Goldenseal, or Yellowroot dropped to 25 cents per pound. Gradually prices improved, but very slowly.

For eleven straight summers, thereafter, my father and I hunted Ginseng and Yellowroot, also, we dug and marketed Mayapple root from May of 1930 through October of 1941.

During those lean years of dire necessity in making a living from the woods in the summertime, I gained my knowledge of these herbs and how to hunt them and prepare them for market. Also, I learned how to find a buyer who would pay the most per pound for dry herbs. In the following pages, I hope to pass onto lovers of the great outdoors a formula that will bring pleasure and financial success to the hunter of herbs if he or she will be diligent and patient in roaming the woods during summertime while hunting for the green gold of hills wild Ginseng and Yellowroot or Goldenseal.

The way you can make up to $50.00 a day or more is in the woods, during summertime in the gathering and marketing of wild Ginseng, Yellowroot, and even Mayapple root. Gather the herbs, wash them, clean them and dry them. Then find a buyer who will pay you the most per pound for your dry herbs. Also, be very sure to find one who will give you honest weight.

First, send to the US Department of Agriculture in Washington D.C and ask them to mail you a farmers' bulletin on the culture of Ginseng and Goldenseal or Yellowroot. The price they ask for their

287

booklet is very low, less than 25 cents usually. This way you will have a booklet on each of these valuable herbs that will give you very valuable information together with some pictures of the herbs.

Now, about Mayapple root. Mostly any old time farmer in rural areas can and will usually point out this herb to you gladly. And most of them will be happy to let you dig in the big patches of this herb out of their pasture fields and woods. Ask the farmers for some grass seed to sow where you dug out the big patches of the Mayapple root. Practically all farmers will be happy to have you show this consideration for this pasture field.

American Ginseng in its wild state grows from 8 to 20 inches high, however some of the old plants grow to 2 feet high and more, then each plant has 3 or more compound leaves, or prongs. Each of these prongs consist of five leaves. But some prongs on young plants have only three leaves. During early summer a cluster of small greenish yellow flowers grow on the seed stem. The seed stem grows up from directly in the center of the prongs. Bright crimson berries with flat seeds therein grow in the place of the flowers later in the summer as time goes by and leaves of the prongs often turn to a golden hue. Then, in late summer, the leaves turn to a bright gold in color.

The root of Ginseng is generally from one half to one inches in thickness. It is spindled shape not unlike a carrot or parsnip and brown to four inches long. Older roots however obtain a much greater length and thickness and are prominently marketed by circular wrinkles. In its wild state, as the years go by, a string of notches from in the neck of the root where the herb grows. To the experienced root hunter, these notches are known in ages, since every notch on the stem of the root represents a year in growth.

Next, familiarize yourself with Ginseng and Yellowroot in its' natural setting. This is very important to the success of any herb gathering venture. If you possibly can, try your best to go out in the woods with an experienced root digger.

By employing this method, you will be able to get much valuable experience and information first hand from one who knows what he is looking for and also where it is likely to be found. This same procedure applies to gathering all herbs. Experience is always the best instrument.

During the early days of my training in the woods, my Father would find a Ginseng plant, then tell me to see if I could find the one he had spotted. At first it was difficult for me, but as time went by, I became so proficient at identifying these herbs especially Ginseng that he and I would usually have a contest going between ourselves to see who could find the most big Ginseng roots during our day in the woods.

If you live in a section of a state where there are mountains covered with forests, especially east of the Mississippi River, bear this in mind, that deep in the heart of these forest of the mountains you will stand a very good chance of finding of wild ginseng root that are worth hundreds and even thousands of dollars. The main thing is to remember in hunting forests of their size is not to get lost in the woods. If you do venture deep into a woods of this size miles from any road or anybody; always have one or more dependable companions with you and a compass. If you do desire, it would probably be to your advantage to have a back pack with each of you. That way you could spend more than one day in the woods without coming out every evening. Also, be sure to have more than one snake bite kit with you.

Remember this always, that persistence pays off in herb gathering just as it does in any other endeavor. Do not expect to become an expert at this sort of thing after your first visit in the woods. Be patient as time goes by. You will call to mind in every new woods you go into where you found the most herbs in other woods you hunted out. Such places are on the tops of banks, real thick weedy or bushy places. These thick places offer excellent cover for the herbs to grow in. Many hunters never venture into these places as they are afraid of snakes. Also, at the tops of the woods and along the edges is another edges is another excellent place to hunt under black walnut trees and butternut trees and mainly on the north and east of hills are usually the best areas to hunt for herbs.

However, and please don't forget this, any woods you may in be this summertime might possibly have herbs in that you would be interested in gathering. So, look them all over carefully because you never can tell when you might happen onto a large clump of aged

Ginseng or a beautiful patch of Yellowroot.

Here is another very important thing to remember, at all times, when you are in the woods during the summertime. Always be on the lookout for herbs and especially Ginseng that every time you find a black walnut tree or butternut tree growing on the poor sides of the hills, there will most almost always be a rich weedy spot around these trees. Look these rich weedy spots over very, very carefully. Always look such in places over very carefully; no matter where you find them in the woods.

In close to a half a century of hunting these herbs, I have found some of my biggest and best herbs in the spots I have just described.

Remember this always and it will reward you handsomely time after time as the summer go by and you hunt out different woods, it always has for me.

Now, a word about digging Ginseng after you find it. Always dig out the herbs in such a way so as to not break up the roots. Every dealer I ever sold to always was more pleased to see the roots whole and unbroken. Also, it also wise to be sure the herbs you sell are washed clean before drying. But do not scrub them. Just make sure they are free of dirt, sticks, stems, small stones and other foreign roots and such. Dealers prefer to buy clean dry herbs.

At the present time, the price per pound for the dry wild Ginseng is at an all time high in the United States. And in Canada, the price per pound for this herb is even higher.

Yellow root or Golden seal is not quite as expensive per pound as it should be right now, considering the price of all other herbs. However, you will find that this herb will add many dollars to the sales you make. So gather it also, every time you find it.

Mayapple root is quite expensive per pound right now. You can make yourself many dollars in the summertime digging and marketing this herb.

Please follow these instructions as I have outlined them and you will succeed. Be patient, be determined to make money and I feel certain you will spend many profitable and enjoyable hours in the woods. I know I have thru the years. Good luck and good hunting.

May God Bless You

Harold H. Milton

1979 -**Janice** and Harold, his first dance.

1972-Giving Janice away at her wedding.

Early 1950's-Jane and Harold

Fall 1969 – Nancy Milton, Janice Blanton and Harold at the park.

Harold Milton

January 16, 1990 – Janice and Harold on her birthday.

1980 – Janice and Harold.

Janice and Harold on Easter.

Janice reviewing Harold's books for publishing.

June, 1986 – Nursing graduation.

Harold's birthday.

Harold at the fireplace in their Bay Village home.

Janice with Harold on his birthday.

Fall, 1969-Jane and Harold.

Harold's grandparents , Alfred Farley and Lucinda Miller Farley.

House on W. 19th – Cleveland, Ohio.

Harold and dog, Heidi.

Harold's birthday

1995 – Harold with great-granddaughter, Madison.

Harold and great-granddaughter

Madison 1996

Harold and daughter, Nancy.

Orville Blanton

\

Janice's Father Orville Blanton

1988 Harold and Janice in the woods.

1993 -Harold gets his GED.

1994 – Harold in Vegas.

Jane and Harold after Nancy's death.

Harold with his GED.

www.ingramcontent.com/pod-product-compliance
Lightning Source LLC
Chambersburg PA
CBHW072205030726
47501CB00015B/651